Kibworth to
A Stroll Down Me   , Lane

Philip J Porter

Kibworth to Smeeton
A Stroll Down Memory Lane

Matador
9 De Montfort Mews
Leicester LE1 7FW, UK
Tel: (+44) 116 255 9311
Email: books@troubador.co.uk
Web: www.troubador.co.uk

ISBN 1 904744 85 0

Cover: St Wilfred's Church, Kibworth (unknown artist c 1887)
Christ Church, Smeeton Westerby (James Smeetin, c 1857)
Many thanks to the owners of the original paintings
for allowing the photographs to be used on the
front cover.

Typesetting: Troubador Publishing Ltd, Leicester, UK
Printed and bound by The Cromwell Press Ltd, Trowbridge, Wilts, UK

Matador is an imprint of Troubador Publishing Ltd

Contents

For my grandson,
Alexander Michael Benjamin Porter.

Acknowledgements

My thanks to Walter Bale, Charles Cooper, and Alonzo Freeland, for taking the original photographs at the time of our tour, without which our memories would be less than complete.

And for the loan of those photographs, Leonard Bromley, Colin Grewcock, Roger Higg, Roger Holt, David Smith, and Rosemary Kent; from the collection of her late husband George.

Some of the photographs were taken later than our stroll, but they do reflect the views of that time, for these my thanks to Alan Davies, Roger Higgs, Roger Holt, David Smith and Diana Wallis from their private collections, with additional photographs from my own collection.

To Mr. G. Arthur, Diana Boulter , Mrs. J. Buxton, Mrs. J. Croxford, Mr. Green, Mr. J. McKean, Mr. M. Mort, Vicki Ryall, Bill Spicknell, Peter Tasker, Mr. R. White, and the many other owners who supplied details on their premises.

To Miss Judy Bale, Leonard Bromley, Kathleen Burrows, Pam Higgs, Roger Higgs, Rose Holyoak, Rosemary Kent, and Jack Waterfield for the additional facts they provided, and to the many Kibworthians, who helped solve many of the undocumented facts.

Many thanks also to the current landowners and farmers for taking the time to provide their field names.

To Robert Gilson for reading the first draft copy, and Lian Smith for proof reading the final copy.

The details in this tour are extracts from my fully referenced Database "Kibworth 1825–1945", itself compiled from: Kibworth & Smeeton's Parish, Vestry, School Records and Documents, Licensing Registers, RDC Plans, Directories. The Census details 1801–1951.

The newspapers between 1811 and 1930, held at the Leicestershire Records Office: The Harborough News, Market Harborough Advertiser, Leicester Advertiser, Leicester Chronicle, Leicester Express, Leicester Guardian, Leicester

Journal & Midland Counties General Advertiser, Leicestershire Mercury, and the Leicester Daily Mercury.

Full acknowledgement is given to the un-named reporters from those newspapers, and their detailed accounts on the news at the time, some from over 190 years ago, without which the history of the villages would have been less than complete.

Many thanks also to the Leicestershire Records Office for allowing the records to be used, and their ever-helpful staff.

With additional details in this book from:

The Railway Museum Research Centre, York.
G. W. Barratt. "A History of Ancient Kibworth"
Bernard Elliott, B.A. "A History of Kibworth Beauchamp Grammar School"
John Nichols. "History and Antiquities of the County of Leicester"
F. P. Woodford. "History of Kibworth"
[1]F. P. Woodford's letters in the Mkt. Harborough Advertiser 1910.
[2]The Enclosure Award. 14 July 1780.
[3]Brian Radford. "Midland Line Memories"
[4]John Gough. "Midland Railway A Chronology"
[5]Lesley Richmond and Alison Turton. "The Brewing Industry"
[6]BT Archives, London
[7]Terrier of Glebe Land belonging to the Parish Church at Kibworth. LRO Ref: 1D 41 /2/351.
[8]Terrier of Glebe Land belonging to the Parish Church at Kibworth. LRO Ref: 1D 41 /2/353.
[9]History of London Institute of Historical Research. "The Victorian History of the Counties of England".
[10]Kibworth Harcourt pre-enclose map. LRO Ref: PP274

Additional notes have been supplied by the owners of their properties in 2003/4. These, and items that are almost certainly correct, but not documented facts are all printed in Italic.

NB. The different spellings of the field names are as they appear on the various documents.

Preface

In compiling my database and this book, with the facts taken from original documents, and not from memories that fade with each passing generation, I have not set out to cover the history of the village, church, chapel and major buildings in depth from the early years, all of which have been covered in previous publications. But to detail the structure of the village during the period mainly from 1780 to 1940, probably the time of greatest change in the three villages, purely to provide the answers to questions which come up from time to time:

What was – when did – or where was so and so...?

So join me in an historical factual tour on Kibworth and Smeeton's History.

Imagine the views that would have confronted you – the people you would meet – and think of the trials and tribulations that faced our forebears as they strove to make the villages what they are today, as you stroll through Newtown, Beauchamp, Harcourt, Smeeton and Westerby, around 1906, and remind ourselves of the events of yesteryear.

Philip J Porter, 2000

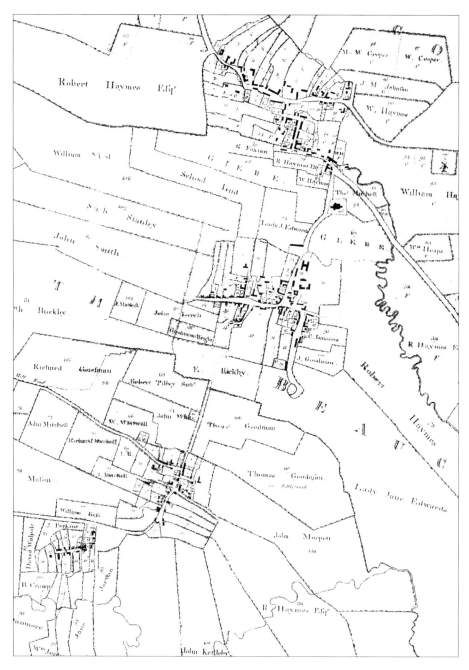

A section of the plan for the Lordships of Kibworth Beauchamp, Kibworth
Harcourt and Smeeton Westerby. 1781.
From a photocopy held by, and courtesy of Leicestershire Records Office.
The original owned by and courtesy of the Warden of Merton Collage, Oxford.

Kibworth and Smeeton Census Totals 1801 - 1951

Year	Beauchamp				Harcourt				Smeeton			
	Total	Male	Female	+/-	Total	Male	Female	+/-	Total	Male	Female	+/-
1801	485				382				365			
1811	555			70	385			3	373			8
1821	588			33	396			11	388			15
1831	604			16	421			25	475			87
1841	748			144	425			4	567			92
1851	733	342	391	-15	466	221	245	41	553	287	266	-14
1861	868	408	460	135	466	214	252	0	533	263	270	-20
1871	1015	511	504	147	474	224	250	8	486	259	227	-47
1881	1123	557	566	108	450	234	216	-24	390	199	191	-96
1891	1003	481	522	-120	460	217	243	10	342	171	171	-48
1901	1157	562	595	154	508	234	274	48	344	165	179	2
1911	1361	645	716	204	446	203	243	-62	336	147	189	-8
1921	1522	711	811	161	435	198	237	-11	302	134	168	-34
1931	1592	749	843	70	520	238	282	85	343	162	181	41
	The Census was not held in 1941 due to the War											
1951	1729	823	843	137	578	244	334	58	321	160	161	-22
	Current estimated population for the villages are:											
2003	3930			2201	1000			422	340			19

Courtesy of ONS

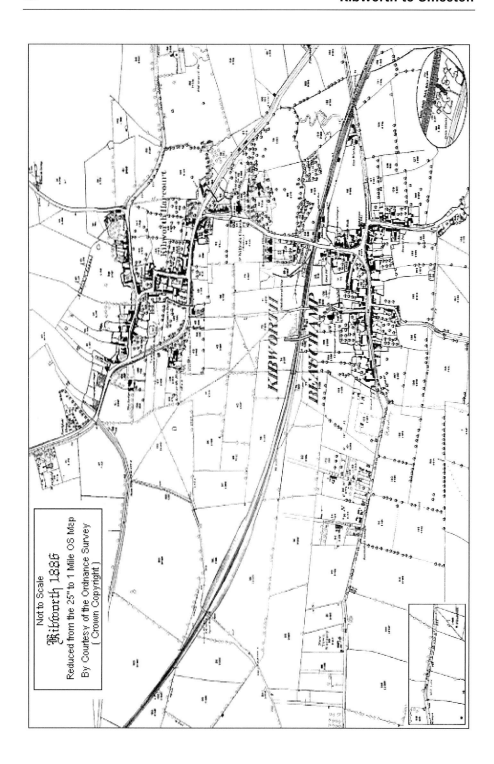

Not to Scale
Kibworth 1886
Reduced from the 25" to 1 Mile OS Map
By Courtesy of the Ordnance Survey
(Crown Copyright)

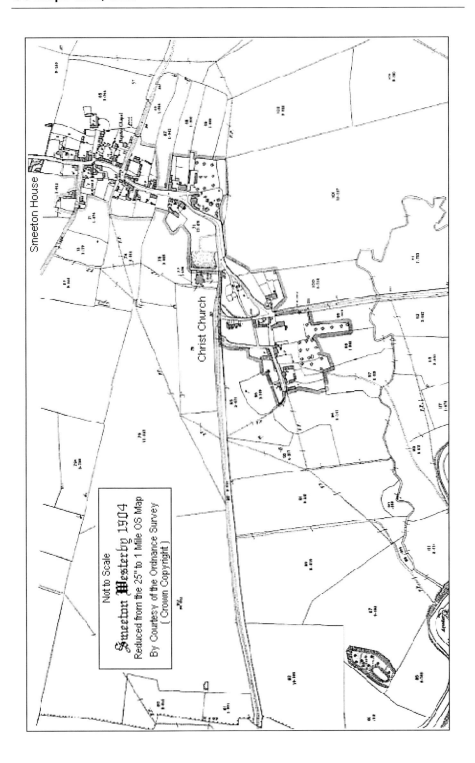

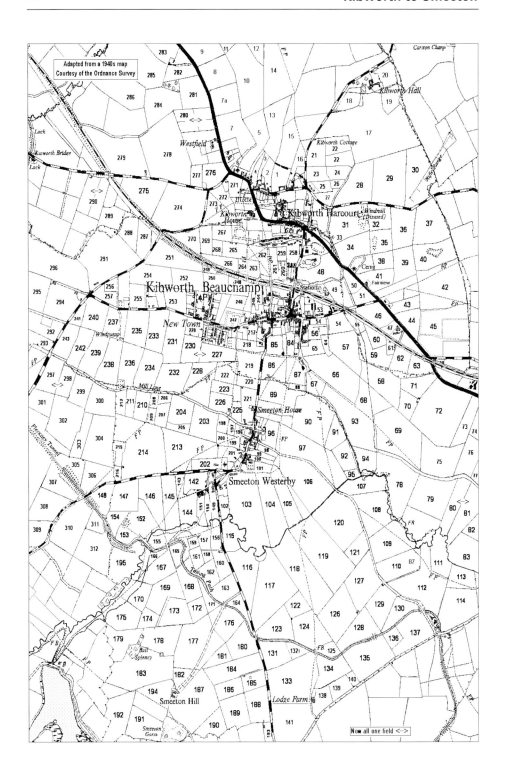

No.	Field Name	*		No.	Field Name	*
1	Fish Pond Close	8		47	Milestone Close	6
2	House Paddock	8		48	Church Hill Close	G
3	Limes Paddock (part)	8		49	Knapp Close	4
4	Limes Paddock (part)	8		50	Drove Close	4
5	Home Close	8		51		
6	The Slang	3		52	Middle Close or Spinney Close	4
7	East Field	8		53	Mason's Home Close	O
8	Seeds	8		54	Home Close (Gas Close. 5)	5
9	Dunkley's	8		55	Little Meadow	6
10	Great Close	3		56		
11	Newland	8		57	Middle Close	5
12	Pen Close	8		58	Cow Close	P
13	Banner	8		59	Big Meadow	5
14	Sharp Sick	3		60	Four Closes	6
15	Gen. Jack's Chestnut	8		61	Little Close (Sewage Works)	6
16	Timms Little Field	8		62		
17	The Park	8		63		
18	Parlour	8		64		
19	Bob's Bottom Paddock	8		65		
20	Bob's Top Paddock	8		66	Wilson Home Close	P
21	Carlton Road Close (Cottage Close)	T		67	Barn Field	P
22	Top Close (Both)	T		68	Home Close Meadow	P
23	Near Four Acres	T		69	Stony Park	P
24	Far Four Acres	T		70		
25	Big Close	T		71	Cricket Meadow	6
26	Far Close	T		72	Nichol's Close	6
27	Slang	T		73		
28	Woman's Dam	8		74		
29	Middle Field	8		75	Sufflands	P
30	Rifle Range	8		76	Tip Field	S
31	Mill Hill	8		77		
32	Thistles	8		78	Westerby Close (First Bass. H)	7
33	Hillbrow (Allotments)	O		79	Second Bass	P
34	Church Hill	8		80	Oak Field (part)	S
35	Spinney Field	8		81	Oak Field (part)	S
36	Short Lees	8		82	Home Paddock	S
37	Long Lees	8		83	19 Acre	S
38	Springs	8		84	Low Ash Close	5
39	Pywell	8		85	(The High School)	
40	Gravel Pit			86		
41	Gravel Close	O		87	Pebberday's Close	6
42	Johnny's Big Field	P		88	Little Meadow	6
43	Football Field	8		89	Cover Close	7
44				90	Narrow Croft (Overtime)	7
45	Pepper (Allotments)	E		91	Owls-Moor Meadow	7
46	Allotments (also Pepper. P)	6		92	Six Acre	7

No.	Field Name	*	No.	Field Name	*
93	Sheep Wash	P	139	Corkley (part)	5
94	Sheep Wash Meadow	P	140	Corkley (part East)	7
95	Fleet Meadow (The Slang)	7	141	Larkley (part)	7
96	Broad Close	1	142	Allen's & Leech's Close	7
97	Stone Bridge Way	7	143	Whitwell Close	7
98	Home Close	6	144	Westerby Close	7
99	Cobly's Home Close (Pear Tree)	7	145	Laundens Close (Whitwers)	7
100	Elliot Croft	7	146	Crooks Acre	7
101	Rev Clark's Paddock	7	147	Blackwell's Close	7
102	Home Close	7	148	Far Feeder	7
103	Millers	V	149	Flaxen	7
104	Whiteland's	7	150	Flaxwell (Flaxen)	6
105	Millers Close	7	151	Workhouse	7
106	The Green	7	152	Stinkley (Red Bank part)	7
107	Owls-Moor (Fleet Meadow)	7	153	Grand Pit Close (Red Bank part)	7
108	First Basses	7	154	Basin Close	7
109	Second Basses	7	155	Mill Dam	7
110	Banwell Close/Meadow	7	156	Brooke Close	V
111	Muck Hill Grove	7	157	Cricket Close	7
112	First Overland (Hoe Furlong)	7	158	Little Close	7
113	Six Cock's (Wigley Meadow)	7	159	Little Arable	6
114	Far Overland	7	160	Miller's Acre	V
115	Little Burgess (Brook Meadow)	7	161	Far Close (Little Meadow)	7
116	Burgess	V	162	Middle Piece	7
117	Big Burgess	7	163	Road Close	7
118	Brook Close	7	164		
119	Plank Close (Top Plank)	7	165	Bentley (The Bend)	7
120	Old Stonebridge (Old Stonebrig)	7	166		
121	Quartern Close	7	167	Buntley	7
122	Stewards Meadow (Hut Meadow)	7	168	Gutteridge Best Close	7
123	The Slade	V	169	Crackley	7
124	Pit Furlong	V	170	Pen Close	7
125	Top Meadow	V	171	Canal Close	7
126	Williams Close	7	172	Gutteridge Meadow	7
127	East Slade	7	173	Over-Moore	7
128	Long Meadow	V	174	Top Close	7
129	Neather Meadow	V	175	West Meadow	7
130	Canal Piece	7	176	Bridge Meadow & Long Meadow	7
131	Topside Close	V	177	Long Hill	7
132	Little Meadow	V	178	Three Bushes	7
133	Larkley (part)	7	179	Stream	7
134	Canal or Bridge Meadow	7	180	Tithe	7
135	Crankland	7	181	Upper Tithe	7
136	Meadow	7	182	Berry-dale	7
137	Streatfield	7	183	Goodman's Barn Close	7
138	West Corkley	7	184	Brickyard Allotment	7

No.	Field Name	*
185	Robsholm (Bottom Brickyard)	7
186	Robsholm (Top Brickyard)	7
187	Barn Close	7
188	Robsholm (part Millers)	7
189	Robsholm (part Millers)	7
190	Little Meadow	7
191	Stopars	7
192	Round Hill	7
193	Bulls Seeds	7
194	Millers	7
195	Watermill Close (Watermill Hill)	1
196	R Haymes. Homestead, etc.	7
197	Ash Close	7
198	Stockwell	7
199		
200	Broad Close (Home Field)	7
201	Masons Close	7
202	Ross's Close (Church Field)	7
203	Brick Kiln Close	7
204	Arable (Siding part)	7
205	Siding	7
206	Top part of Mill Field	7
207	Burrows Close (Mill Field)	7
208	Mill Yard (Mill Field)	7
209	Mill Garden	7
210	Willow Close (Millers Close. 7)	K
211	Allen's First Close (Hill Close)	7
212	Allen's Second Close	7
213	Drawstone	7
214	Larkley	7
215	Larkley Meadow	7
216	Saddington Rectory Field	7
217		
218		
219	Lower Delcus	V
220	Delcas One	K
221	Banbury First Close	7
222	Delcas Two (Hut Close)	K
223	Top Close/Field	M
224	Stud Paddock	M
225	Farm Field	M
226	Whitwell (Mill Field. M)	7
227	Middle Delcus (Top Delcus)	V
228	Cow Pasture	7
229	(The Cricket Field to 2005)	
230	Mill Gutter	V

No.	Field Name	*
231	Hammer Head	D
232	Thistles	V
233	Football Field	P
234	Behind Football Field	P
235	Wire Fence Filed	P
236	Cottage Field	P
237	Cow Shed Field	P
238	Mill Field Fleckney	P
239		
240	Wire Field	P
241		
242	Lambing Field	P
243	Sub Field	P
244	Bridge Close	W
245	Bridge Field	O
246		
247	Pump Close	O
248	Spring Hill (Johnny's Brook)	W
249		
250	Second Field	P
251	Lower Great Close	P
252	Third Field	P
253		
254	Top Field	P
255	Radical	P
256		
257	Tory	P
258		
259		
260		
261		
262	School Back Close	G
263		
264		
265		
266	Colwell (Long Meadow. 8)	P
267		G
268	Close	G
269		
270	Great Close	P
271	Lodge Close	O
272	Dairy Close	8
273		
274	Crindle Dyke (Cryndle Dyke. O)	8
275	Black Hut	8
276	Town End Lees	6

No.	Field Name	*	No.	Field Name	*
277			295	Hovel	P
278	Top Seed	8	296	25 Acre Long Field	P
279	Old Golf Course	8	297		
280	The Glebe	8	298		
281	Debdale	8	299	Cox's Meadow	H
282	Spinney Close	8	300	The Seeds	H
283	Turnpike Seeds	8	301	Tunnel Field	H
284	Middle Close	8	302	Limba Hill	H
285	Carter's	8	303	Narrow Limba	H
286	Conscience	8	304	Big Limba	H
287	Sandercocks	8	305	Barn Field	H
288	Far Close	P	306	Bridge Meadow	H
289	Bush Close	P	307	Football Field	H
290	Newlands	9	308	Under Hill	H
291	Rutwell	8	309	Townsend Hill (or Bull Beds)	H
292	Top Filed	W	310	Pen Close	H
293	Big Moss	W	311	Basin Meadow	H
294	First Field	P	312	Plough Field	H

* Source for post-enclosure field names. The earliest known name is shown with its
source, a later name and possible a different source is included in brackets.

1: Kibworth & Smeeton Enclosure Award 1780
2: Estate of Mr. Needham 1850. LRO Ref: 3042/M68
3: Land belonging to Edward Wright Gimson. DE 389 MA/161/1, (document undated)
4: Estate of Robert Haymes 1918. Courtesy of Joan Spain
5: Robert Haymes Schedule of Properties 1894. Courtesy of Ian Windridge
6: Estate of R Bryan Haymes 1918
7: Field Name Survey for Smeeton WI. Ref: FNs/295/1 1a, 2. By F Aggas & G Yates 1967-68,
   the names supplied by Peter Higgs, Mr. S. Cooley, Mr. Rammel, Mr. R. Watson, and Mr. Vendy
8: Mrs. Janet Briggs, Mr. M. Stops, Mr. D. Briggs, Mr. J. Briggs.
D: Mrs. D. Welton
E: Mrs. J. Exley, Mrs.J Spain, Bill Stanbridge
G: Glebe Land at Kibworth
H: Richard Harrison
K: Mrs. P. Kenney
M: Mr. J. Mckean
P: Pam Higgs, from a map compiled by her late husband, Peter Higgs
S: Mark Stanbridge
T: John Timms
V: Mrs. E. Vickers
W: Jack Waterfield
O: Other Miscellaneous Documents.

NB. On the accompanying field map, certain streets have been deleted to show the original field
    boundary.

The Start of the Tour

Fleckney Rd. c 1930, in the far distance would have been the second field gate out of the village.

So our historical factual tour starts on Saturday 26 May 1906, but to be precise and refresh our memories on the facts faced by our ancestors, we shall travel through the passage of time from the late 1700s to that most regrettable deed in 1968.

We meet just past Gladstone St., at the far end of Kibworth Cricket Club's ground, where the second of the field gates on the dirt road to Fleckney stands, leaning on that while glancing further along to the bend in the road – at the third gate, you notice the hive of activity at Newtown Nursery.

Just beyond that - on the adjoining allotment, the bungalow built in 1911 for C. W. Cooper, one of Kibworth's main photographers at the time of our tour, while the sub-postmaster in Beauchamp.

Kibworth Cricket Club c 1955, and their first timber Pavilion. Prior to this, one of the "Beaconsfield Cottages" (built in 1877) opposite the ground, was used as their changing room, ironically where many cricket balls have since passed through its windows over the years.

As we turn around to start our stroll, Kibworth's Cricket Club's first eleven are batting in a match against one of their old rivals, on the ground where they have played since the 1884 season, this being the second field the present club, have, and would play on until the end of the 2005 season.

The earliest records of a Cricket Club at Kibworth date from 1847, but it is possible they only played until 1850. The club then re-formed in May 1857, and continued without a break until 1871. Then after a possible break of one year in 1872, the present club have played continuously since the start of the 1873 season.

In the South-west corner of their ground, near the corner gate, stands the timber pavilion, built in 1898, by Mr Branston, a well known builder and carpenter at that time and assisted by Robert Holt, carpenter, of Smeeton, both also coffin makers in the village.

The advert for the show, as it appeared in the "Midland Mail".

KIBWORTH AND SMEETON HORTICULTURAL SOCIETY'S

ANNUAL SHOW

Will be held at KIBWORTH

ON SATURDAY, AUG 19, 1899.

On the

CRICKET GROUND. FLECKNEY ROAD.

THE HARBOROUGH VOLUNTEERS BAND.

DANCING ON THE GREEN.

COCONUTS ALLEYS.

REFRESHMENTS BY MR. LYNN.

CRICKET MATCH,
                    KIBWORTH v LUTTERWORTH.

GATES OPEN 2 O'CLOCK.

GEORGE LYNN
F. J. LOVEDAY } Hon Secs.

The cricket field was also used for the first time by the Kibworth and Smeeton Horticultural Society for their show in August 1899, when two large marquees were erected to accommodate the exhibits, but in order not to encroach on the playing space; one was erected in the adjoining field loaned for the occasion by Mr. Hulland. One attraction was a cricket match between KCC and Lutterworth, the visitors bringing the County Captain Mr. C. Marriott, the result: Lutterworth; 107, Kibworth; 94 for 9.

Beauchamp's celebrations went ahead there on June 26th 1902, to mark the Crowning of King Edward VII. He had been taken ill two days previously, but requested that the celebration went ahead, a marquee capable of seating 600 people was filled to overflowing at one o'clock for dinner. The children attending the National School assembled there at 3 o'clock, when each received a medal, and were then marched to the field for tea at 4 o'clock. A programme of sports took place followed by dancing until half-past ten. With a balance in hand from the June festivities, the original programme was repeated on Saturday August 9th, the re-arranged day of his Coronation, when the Great Glen Brass Band provided the music.

Similar celebrations also took place in Harcourt in Mr. Wright's field, where all the children were presented with mugs; the Wigston United Band provided the music. While Smeeton celebrated the occasion in Mr. Hunt's field and the children each received a medal.

Moving on – as we stroll down the road by the side of the ground, which – although the kerb stones had been laid in 1902, the pavements and the road itself were still just dirt tracks - like the remainder of the roads in the two villages, waiting to be "tarred", and think how lucky our walk hadn't taken place five years ago in a dry period, before the sewers in Newtown and elsewhere were constructed, when the open-ditches were used as the outfalls for the disposal of the sewage from the old brick culverts, and there would have been an offensive smell that persisted in summer, not only along this; but quite a few of the other open-ditches that ran beside the roads, waiting for a period of heavy rain to flush them.

Fleckney Rd. in 1905, with only three houses in sight, until we reach the off licence.

Then glance into the pond situated just downhill from the North-east corner of the cricket field - near the tree. Opposite that, you notice how imposing and out of place the factory belonging to Johnson & Barnes and built around 1897, looked on the corner of Dover Street.

J & B, Fleckney Rd. c 1905, the shadows suggest the workers are
on their way home for lunch.

Just as we become aware of how well Kibworth's bell-ringers; practising at St. Wilfred's Church sound in the distance, a shout came from the cricket field with the visiting team claiming their first wicket; a "duck".

On the right past the factory - none of the streets existed, with the first of the houses just starting to be built on Fleckney Rd., and your view would have been across open fields towards Mill Lane.

While on the left past the factory, only three houses existed before we arrive at the open field, where later on Saturday the 9 July 1921, after members had contributed sums of £50 or £100 toward the cost, the new Kibworth Working Men's Club was opened, built on land owned by the United Order of Oddfellows (prior to this the members used a timber shed on the adjoining land) and members were able to enjoy their "modest pint" there for the first time. At that time, Harry Billing was the first President of the newly opened club, and presided at the weekly Sunday evening lectures in the concert room on the Labour Party, one entitled "The Goal." Then as we return to our tour, the only other house at the time was the outdoor beer house, owned by William Smith.

When we arrive there, we pause and think of the bewilderment there in the past, when first in February 1879, the Liberal Land Society originally named the streets on their three estates as: The two streets on No. 1 estate, were named Dover St. & Gladstone St., one in No. 2 estate as High St., and four in No. 3 estate as Bright St., Gold St., Silver St., and Peel St., although later in 1886, only the outline of these are shown on the map.

Later the Parish Council had other thoughts on these, and on 10 July 1900 they named the streets that were to be built on "Pump Close" as: Buller St., Kimberley St., Roseberry Ave., and the street at the far end of these, White St., which, at their previous meeting in April - they proposed to name it Highcross St.

Moving on to the junction with Roseberry Ave., we make a detour across the two fields at the bottom of the avenue to view the new timber "Tin Bridge", which, after many years of trying the Midland Railway Co., due to the extra people crossing the line after the opening of the factory on Fleckney Rd., finally agreed in August 1903 to throw a bridge over the level crossing, removing the public danger and which proved to be a great advantage to the village.

Helen Cooke, on the old Wooden Bridge, c 1922, replaced by the new Tin Bridge, after the slow line was opened on 17 November 1926.

To the North-west of the bridge and just prior to the Warwick Road Bridge, the first North Signal Box can be seen on the embankment there, until it was moved to far side of the bridge when the track was widened. Then glance down the line to the next bridge – standing complete over the line, and beyond that – the School Road Bridge.

Retracing our steps, as we re-cross "Johnny's Brook"; named after John Waterfield who farmed the land at the time and see the abundant supply of watercress in the brook, evidence itself of the sandy soil in the villages, and make a mental note to return later to pick some, and hoping we wouldn't be caught in the process. The brook is no longer there.

Arriving back at the junction of Roseberry Ave. and Fleckney Rd., at the point where the first field gate out of the village stands – on the boundary between Beauchamp and Newtown, which later in 1925 the Rural District Council would remove along with the remainder of the field gates still standing, and enclose the road from Kibworth to Fleckney at a cost of £295.

We pause, and opposite – the vacant plot on a winters day – after fall of snow, and the site where the "Empire Hall" would be built in 1913. To the right of the photo at the end of the neat hedge row and palisade fencing, the stile at the start of the footpath leading to Mill Lane can just be seen, the road at the time still unmade; with the kerb stones waiting to be laid.

The "Empire Hall", c1930, shortly after the road had been adopted.

In 1908, G. W. Barratt advertised as a "Dealer in Rare Books. Kibworth Beauchamp. Valuation of Libraries Undertaken", a year later he also became an agent for Ian Coope & Co. Brewery for their good sound ale at 8d per gallon, he sold these from his grocer's shop at 45 High St., (the houses were not numbered in Kibworth until 1935, and in the 1960s at Smeeton, but have been added for clarification) and used a large workshop at the rear to repair the antiques he also dealt in.

Later in 1911 - he published his book the "History of Ancient Kibworth". Then in 1913 he became the tenant of the newly built "Empire Hall", and moved his antiques business there while still keeping his grocery shop, until c 1930.

The building was first erected for Cinema shows, but these were only given on certain nights of the week, in 1914 - he applied and was granted a theatrical license for the hall, to hold theatrical shows on other nights of the week, although it is uncertain if any such shows actually occurred. *From the start, apparently his antique chairs were used for the seating at the film shows.*

While next to the hall, stands "Southlands", built around 1901/2.

Leaving the new part of the village still known as Newtown behind us, we enter High Street, (which, was originally known as Main St., before it was re-named at the same council meeting in 1900, probably to avoid it being confused with Main St., in Harcourt), and arrive at the old thatched farmhouse – the last occupants being Amos Cooke and his family, until he retired around 1936. On the left hand side of the farmyard gateway and built into the wall, was the last post box before leaving the village – which remained there until the late 1940s.

A view looking down High St, c 1945, from where the first field gate
to Fleckney, stood until 1925.

High St., c 1918.

On the left, only partly visible on this photo, the farmhouse which was demolished in the 1970s, and nearly opposite that – the thatched cottage that met a similar fate in 1947, apart from one remaining mud wall adjoining the footpath.

Beyond the farmhouse and standing back from 75 High St. – the last of four cottages, stands the original pair of cottages – numbers 73 and 71, these were certainly in existence before 1885 and would be demolished later around 1969. While further down on the left you pass "Elms Farm" and the adjacent Co-op store, both

73 High Street   71 High Street

built in 1900/1. Perhaps from when it first opened, but certainly shortly afterwards, the store consisted of a butcher's shop on the left and grocery department
on the right, with a bakery at the rear of the premises. The farmhouse was demolished on 27 and 28 July 2004, to expand the store.

Next to which was the entrance to a farmyard and now a car park for the store,
and beyond that, the building originally known as "Beauchamp Hall" and used by
the Baptists for a place of worship from October 1885 until 1924. The building
was then used by St. Wilfred's as a church hall for a number of years.

High St., and "The Royal Oak", c 1935

Further down at 36a and 38 – would be the "Royal Oak" – kept by William Brutnell, next door to the present post office. Later, when George B. Holyoak was the Innkeeper at the "Oak", the Northampton Brewery Co., the owner's of the Inn, extinguished the licence for the sale of intoxicating liquer on evening of the 30 September 1958.

Pausing outside the Inn, we reflect on the location of one of Kibworth's "Extinct Inn's" – the Halford Arms, which had closed by 1842.

In 1901 – at the next house to the Royal Oak lived Robert Roberts, a shoemaker, (although his shop was next to the thatched cottage in School Lane), then Samuel Rudkin; butcher, W. Smith; grocer, another butcher the London Meat Co., and then Alfred Dalton; shoemaker. To the left of the Inn was a book seller and newsagents run by Walter Hare, then Priscilla Simonds; florist and grocer on the corner of the road to Smeeton. Opposite the Inn was George Barratt's grocery shop, and next door a fishmonger and fruitier.

Since June 1905 at least, Harry Cox and his son John – were green grocers on High St., the exact location unclear, but according to "G. W. Barratt" later in 1911 – Mr. H. Cox lived at the Halford Arms. So the Inn would have been one of the grocery/fruit shops.

At the time of our tour, the three villages were blessed with five grocery shops, three fishmongers/fruitier, four butchers, and eleven other shopkeepers - with some of these also selling groceries and fruit, and a baker in each village. Your milk was delivered direct from the many farms in the villages, with some of the farmers delivering their milk twice a day. With the many grocers and greengrocers in the village - competition was pretty fierce, especially so when some of the smaller ones - to help the locals, started selling produce they had the audacity (according to others who threatened them with legal action unless they ceased) - to import goods purchased on the nearby markets, instead of just their own home produced, although those complaining were already agents for the large combines of the day.

The Thatched Cottage on the corner of School Rd.,
until it was demolished in 1959.

On the left hand corner of School Lane, re-named in 1900 to School Road, stands another thatched cottage, and still referred to by elder Kibworthians as "Daisy Drivers", the last occupant as a haberdashery shop, and on the opposite corner a barber, and bakery shop.

As we are about to set off up School Rd., someone amongst our followers, remarks: "Hang on – you've forgotten to mention Blondin!", but one look placed in his direction – silenced the enthusiastic looks from the remainder of the party.

Then glance back down to Hare's stationers and newsagents, before strolling past the Wesleyan Methodist Church – opened in 1846, and the cottages next to it.

Next to that, behind the high brick wall after 1929, would have been the Grammar School tennis courts. Then the school itself, erected in 1725 to replace the first school that used to stand 50 yards further down towards the railway in Kilpeck's Close, it built around 1630, and according to an ancient myth - a tunnel ran under one of the schools, probably the first, from the "Manor House" and up to St Wilfred's, which in all probability was just an old brick culvert that the school governors had blocked up in 1891, in the basement of the second school.

Opposite the school – the sand pits that used to occupy the site down to where the Railway Arms Inn now stands, then we continue down the lane, through the swing gates, until we reach the uppermost part of the bridge.

Pausing on the brow of the bridge, where, if you had been in the same position, or to be precise 15 feet below the brow, for the first five years or so after the railway opened, you would have been standing in the middle of a level crossing, and imagine how the "Little End Sidings", "Gully hole", "Villas", and St Wilfred's, looked in the distance.

Re-tracing our steps, and as we reach High St., I was just thinking to myself that thankfully I had avoided the subject, again came the request: "But – what about Blondin?" So!

Blondin

Just in case any of your party were unaware of the request, the gentleman in question was supposed to have visited Kibworth at some point, and according to Francis P. Woodford (baptised 17 January 1861,) in his book the *History of Kibworth*, that when a Mr. Staines kept the Royal Oak, he states: "It was from the roof of this house, to that of one of the houses opposite, that Blondin had a rope stretched, on which he walked blindfolded, wheeled a barrow across; and also on which he balanced a stove and cooked a pancake, which he tossed in the air, to the thrills and wonder of a great crowd below – but to only a small addition to his purse. Many free displays of juggling, etc. took place..."

Unfortunately he did not give a date when this occurred – or even which house it was stretched across to, but Mr. Staines was not at the "Royal Oak" at the time of 1861 Census, taken on April 7th, and a new Publican was at the Inn by 1866. The only record of him at the Inn is in a Directory of 1863, probably compiled the previous year.

The background to the request over – now the facts: Charles Blondin, was born "Jean Francios Gravelet"; 1824-1897, a French acrobat. He first crossed Niagara Falls on a tightrope in 1859, a feat he repeated a few times. While returning after his performance there, he toured England and Ireland, but why Kibworth?

M. Blondin made his first appearance at the Crystal Palace on Saturday 1 June 1861. His feats were mentioned in the House of Commons, the following Monday, when a member asked the Home Secretary, if he knew that Blondin had introduced a child of tender years in his dangerous exploits. Having confirmed this – he felt it his duty to write to the directors of the palace conveying to them a warning on the subject, and he trusted that communications would have the effect of preventing a renewal of the performance.

Amongst his other appearances were at the Derby Arboretum on Friday 12 July 1861, and at Aston Park, Birmingham, on 13 July 1861, when in spite of the rain, there were no less than 80,000 persons present.

Charles Blondin c 1859

He appeared at the Crystal Palace again for one performance only on July 24th at the Brass Band Contest, when the Admission was Half-a-Crown. (For the rest of the contest it was a shilling.)

The Midland Railway Co. placed an advert, which states: Blondin at Nottingham, on Tuesday July 30th. An excursion train will leave Rugby, Mkt. Harborough, and Leicester, and intermediate stations for Nottingham. It departs Kibworth at 9.32a.m., and returns from Nottingham at 7.00p.m., with the fare of 4s 0d for 1st class, and 2s 6d for 2nd class, from all stations.

He appeared at Dublin on the 14th and 15th of August 1861, and at Belfast on the 16th and 17th of August.

On November 2nd, Stevens's New Circus, perform at the Fleur-de-lis-ground, Belgrave Gate, Leicester. Mrs. Hudson – the celebrated Female Blondin will appear nightly in her extraordinary performance on the tight rope. (She appeared there for only the first week, although the circus was there for a further five.) The report on her performance, states: "The Female Blondin in her daring walk on the tight rope at an altitude of above 35 feet is a performer which should be witnessed to be believed."

On Friday 15 November 1861, Howe's celebrated Anglo-American Circus, with their troupes of equestrians, acrobats, etc., visited Harborough and gave two performances in the paddock of Mr. Jas. Bennett, of the Cherry Tree Inn before each performance, the celebrated Female Blondin made her ascent on the rope from the ground to the top of the pavilion, which astonished all onlookers. At night her usual assent was illuminated. Tom Sayer's and Hame's American Circus also visited the town.

It appears thought that there was at least one male impersonator, for in February 1862, a fatal accident occurred, when a boy lost his life at an exhibition given by Mr Duvalli, who calls himself the English Blondin at South Shields.

In a Court case at York on 3 May 1862, two men were before the court after speculating in Blondin, when he exhibited in Ireland on four days in 1861. They refused to pay their dues, owing to bad weather, he claimed they had agreed to pay him £130, and £160 if he appeared twice at the same venue – on the same day, he won the case for the balance due.

An advert in a paper informs us that: "Blondin at Charnwood Forrest. Mr. Sharp Tugby begs to inform the Public that he has, at enormous expense, made arrangements for the world renowned Blondin, to give one of his astonishing performances on the Cricket Ground, Whitwick, on July 1st 1862, Military Bands, Dancing, and other amusements."

After finding the above I contacted a member of Whitwick History group, who, until then – knew of the legend of his appearance there, but not the location and date. But apparently the village blacksmith made the chains and handcuffs for Blondin's "Escape from a mail sack", these hung in the Inn the Tugby family built and owned "The Blacksmith Arms", until that closed in 1908. The chains were then moved to the Smithy's, where they hung on the back wall until they were requisitioned for the war effort in 1940. The Cricket ground was sold to the Whitwick Burial Board in 1876, and later became the Whitwick Cemetery.

So feeling rather chuffed with myself at solving the mystery of the Frenchman's visit to Whitwick for them, we toil hopefully on – to solve his alleged visit here.

CAMPBELL-STREET GROUNDS.
NEAR THE RAILWAY STATION, LEICESTER.

ON THURSDAY and FRIDAY, SEPTEMBER 11th and 12th, (the two Race Days), BLONDIN'S first and last appearance in Leicester, previous to his departure for the Court of St. Petersburg. The World renowned

BLONDIN,
THE HERO OF NIAGARA,
ON THE HIGH ROPE PERFORMANCE,

THE SAME AS HE APPEARED IN BEFORE HIS ROYAL HIGHNESS THE PRINCE OF WALES AT THE FALLS OF NIAGARA.

There will be a Grand Display of FIREWORKS each Evening, such as has never been witnessed in Leicester before by Professor WILDER, of the Royal Vauxhall Gardens, Birmingham. For particulars see programme.

YOUNG WILDER

Will give his extraordinary performance on the Flying Trapeze.

MONS. TOURNAIN,

The great Dragon Tamer, will make his Terrific Flight across the Ground at an elevation of seventy feet. The Illumination of the Grounds will be of the most novel and brilliant description during the evening. There will, at intervals, be given Vocal and Instrumental Concerts, Balloon Ascents, &c., &c.

Four MILITARY BANDS are engaged for the occasion.

Arrangements have been made by all the Railway Companies to run Cheap Trains. Excursionists admitted at half-price by showing their Railway Ticket. No Train will leave Leicester until after Blondin's performance.

There will be a platform erected by Mr. Stirk to accommodate 2,000 persons. To prevent inconvenience at the gates, the public are requested to purchase Tickets before the evenings of the Feats. Tickets to be had at all the Newspaper Offices, and other places appointed by the Committee.

Entrance for the Reserved Seats. Fox-street and Northampton-street, 1s. 6d. Campbell Entrance, 1s. After Blondin's Performance, admission for the Fireworks and Concert, 6d. each.

Refreshments will be provided on the Grounds by Mr. C. INMAN, Princess Charlotte Inn.

Advert for Blondin's appearance at Campbell Street, Leicester, on the 11th and 12th September 1862.

The report on his performance at Leicester paper state: "The hero of the tight-rope, the celebrated Blondin, has visited Leicester this week, and given performances on the two race-days, in a large enclosed piece of ground to the north of Campbell Street. On Thursday evening he commenced about half-past six o'clock, and his performance lasted until seven. He went through his usual feats. First he walked and run across the rope (Which was about the thickness as a man's wrist). Returning he wheeled a barrow over. Next he blindfolded himself, placed a bag over his head reaching nearly to his feet, and in this apparently helpless state went on the rope. Several feints of missing the line, and other tricks, proved that he was as much at home on his narrow route, as others on the ground, so as to remove the slightest apprehension of any danger to him in his performance. At the middle he lay down on his back and got up again. Divesting himself of his muffling on reaching the end of the rope, he returned to the middle backwards. He then fastened his pole to the rope, left it some distance, and performed several feats, such as hanging by the arms and the legs, turning over forwards and backwards, swimming, standing upright with his arms folded, etc. He then returned to the end of the rope and concluded his performance by carrying a man on his back. His successful exhibition was greeted with enthusiastic applause.

After the conclusion of his performance a number of feats of strength and agility were performed by young Wilders, and entertainments of the evening were concluded by a fine exhibition of fireworks by Mr. Wilders. The Militia Band and the Loughborough Rifle Band performed during the evening, the attendance was numerous, and no doubt the speculation would prove a profitable one.

★ ★ ★

With that I assume his performances in England came to an end.

So did he, and if so – when and why did Blondin come to Kibworth to perform in the Main St.?

Where did they secure the rope – which according to the reports, was about two and a half inches in diameter, between the two buildings in Main Street, the "Royal Oak", and one of the houses opposite, and would the buildings, and most probably, the chimneys, stand the strain ?

When he was getting £130 for each performance, and £160 if he appeared twice at the same venue on the same day, and it cost "at enormous expense" for him to perform at Whitwick?

★ ★ ★

If he did so, then it certainly would have been between the census in 1861, and his performance at Leicester, when it states that it is his last performance before his departure to the Court of St Petersburg, and most likely – between his visit to Whitwick on 1 July 1862, and around his Leicester performance, on the 11th and 12th of September 1862.

★ ★ ★

By now all our tour party, wishing they hadn't brought the subject up – stifling a yawn – non the wiser – move on.

Clock Tower to Weir Road

Continuing our tour – you glance down Smeeton Lane at "Victoria House", and what was until it was re-named in 1900 the end of Smeeton Lane and the start of Victoria St.

Victoria House, c 1960. Demolished c 1973, for and prior to the straightening of the road.

Prior to this, at one time and for many years, the whole length of the road leading to Smeeton was named Victoria St., apparently so-named many years earlier – after a Mr. Charles Bryant, a highly respected and popular tradesman who was endowed with a high sense of patriotism, and at the National Holiday in 1837 to celebrate the marriage of the late Queen Victoria, took advantage of it by painting Victoria's name on the corner of the house.

High St., pre 1913.

Opposite Smeeton Rd. stands "Beauchamp House", or "Beauchamp House School", as it was for some years around 1860 to 1880, when a Mr. Durham ran a middle class school there for young Gentlemen.

Later, it was the home of W. W. Underwood, where, for around 5 years until 1885, the Baptists held services – either in the house or the large outbuilding adjacent to the road, then moving their Chapel to "Beauchamp Hall" on High St.

The same building to the right of Beauchamp House, which adjoins the road, was opened on the 11 November 1942 as Kibworth's British Restaurant, to feed the needy and evacuees at Kibworth during the second World War, and catering for 100 meals a day, when its set menu was: Meat & Veg.; 8d, Sweet; 3d, Soup; 2d, and Tea; 1d. There was no charge for meals served to schoolchildren, and it closed as a restaurant around the end of 1946.

Resuming our tour, before we pass the "Manor House", where, at that time, there was a wall completely around the front and side, we pause and think how well an ornamental chiming clock on top of a tower would look and sound, in a prominent position on the corner of the outbuildings there, and long-standing Kibworthians later came to appreciate, when one was erected, above where previously the town pump stood, just down from the corner, which in 1873, after standing useless for many years was sold by auction, and the well covered by a slab.

If we had been strolling down to the "Bank" one year later – in August 1874, one of the free shows that used to entertain our ancestors was in progress, and this can only be left to the local reporter of the time to describe, who wrote: "Dog and Monkey Entertain. On Saturday a large crowd of people was attracted to the "Bank" by some instrumental music (if this is not a misnomer for what was heard) discarded in a manner which led to the belief that the performers, if not entirely capable of appreciating the beauties of the crescendo and diminuendo were thorough masters of the fortissimo style. Indeed so powerful and discordant were the

The occasion unknown, but with the single lamp on the "Bank", it is pre 1898.

vibration of the humid air that the musically sensitivity were momentarily threatened with chronic deafness and the by no means pleasant sensation of their teeth being set on edge. The subsequent performances were, however, of a much superior and widely different character. The feats of Blondin were performed by a Monkey in a remarkably "elegant" manner. Jacko also donned the garb of a coachman, and mounted the box of a miniature carriage to which were attached two dogs, which pulled him round the stage in proper style, and it was wondrous to see the dignity Jacko assumed in this position, and how dextrous he managed the reins and flourished the whip over the backs of the animals. Indeed so intuitively clever did this quadrumanous creature appear to be that apparently, but very little more was needed to convert many of the tickled spectators to the Darwinian doctrine."

On reaching "The Bank" at the time of our tour, but was previously known as "The Cross Bank" and prior to 1825 "The Green". The house (16) on the left should be another of Kibworth's closed Inn's, The Half Moon, this to – had closed before 1842.

High St., from the "Bank", c 1905.

In the distance, standing in front of the "Manor House", can be seen the building where Kibworth's first Fire Engine was housed, then on the right of the street, the walled garden – with its walnut trees in the centre, but where plans are well advanced for the building of a school there. The council had already received 13 tenders for the erection of same, which ranged from £1,449 15s to £2,030, and opened in 1907.

While along Paget St., the Liberal Club built c 1875, and on the right hand corner of the street (which, before the parish council re-named the roads in 1900, was Gladstone St., and in all probability the reason there were two streets with the same name – was because the new part of the village – at that time – was still known and thought of as a "Newtown", and not part of Beauchamp) – stands the house, built for the Headmaster of the National School in 1873 by Mr. J Mason for £357 15s,

Paget St., the Schoolmasters house, and National School, c 1905.

and occupied at the time of our tour, and until 2 years after he retired at the end of the summer term of 1910, by Mr. Alfred Cooper, who was also the parish clerk.

According to the Electoral Register, he moved to "Rectory Cottage", in the 12 months after October 1911, but according to "Barratt" when compiling his book in late 1910, Mr Cooper; schoolmaster, lived in another of Kibworth's extinct Inn's – the Bird in the Hand. I just cannot see that the schoolhouse was the Inn Barratt referred to, unless he was referring to a previous house that is shown there on the 1780 enclosure map.

On the right of his house – the boys' playground and the National School – built in 1842 after tenders submitted ranged from £448, to the lowest and except-ed one from J. Mason of Kibworth for £380. While opposite that stands the village hall.

The shops on "Station Corner", c 1918.

Facing you would be G. Lynn's shop, to its right William Willey, saddler there until c 1914, then later and for many years owned by Edmond Leach and his son, then the shop on the right of the row, was another grocer's shop, owned at the time by Tom Branston, who built the cricket pavilion, and some of the repair work at the St. Wilfred's, with his carpenters shop and saw-mills at the rear, the shop later run by my Aunt Doris in the 1930s. Standing back from the corner was Hare's, the drapers, and the end of the Old Swan.

"The Bank", c 1905.

To your right, the road sign on the wall above the grocer's shop window, informs us that you were on "Station Corner", and your attention is then drawn to the Diamond Jubilee Memorial Lamp in the centre, finally erected after many debates in 1898, with "Cross Bank House" to its right.

Just as we glance across "The Bank", we move forward in time to the autumn of 1910, and who should join our tour but F. P. Woodford, who, although living in Leicester, was visiting his birthplace, so he describes the scene for us here in the 1820s, when his father, Job Bull Woodford, (born 1813) – was a child:

"The "Cross Bank" was not only the market place on which the weekly market, granted by Henry III., to be held on Monday, but the place on which the Statute Fair was held annually for the "Hiring of servants," and also the site on which the annual gathering called Kibworth Wrestling, was held; when wrestlers exhibited their skill, which – according to my father's account – consisted principally of "kicking each others naked shins" with their feet, which were encased in heavy boots, generally rendered as hard as possible by being seeped in "bullock's blood" for some months, and afterwards dried in the sunlight. It was also the scene of many bull baiting, and other brutal sports."[1] With that – he left – for us to resume our tour and back in time.

For many years, at the time of the village feast, held on the last Monday and

Tuesday of October the stalls, shooting galleries and other attractions had been on the "Cross Bank", but from 1867, the bank and roads were so crowded that horses and vehicles could not pass without danger to the pedestrians, and finally in 1877 the site for the feast was moved to the field opposite the Rose and Crown.

In 1887 after a petition of the villagers, who were loosing out financially with this – and especially so the Innkeepers, the annual feast, returned to the Bank and Weir Lane, although as usual the crowds – and usually referred to at that time as "influx of our cousins", started to arrive in the village on the Sunday morning and stayed for the duration, and later in 1893, two Home Fields were rented from Mr. E. Mason, for Neal's galloping Horses, Twigdon's galloping horses and rolling ships, and Proctor's Circus. Another attraction was Edison's Phonograph, which he invented in 1877 and still quite a novelty, the fortunate owner doing a very good business. On the Monday evenings of the feast the Brass Band held their usual ball at the Village Hall. Although by 1895, moves were already underway prohibiting shows, and standings on the Bank.

"The Old Swan", c 1907.

Moving down to get a frontal view of the Old Swan Inn, your host there at the time was Tom Coleman. When Mr. W. Fletcher a previous host presided there between 1870 and 1891, his business had improved so by 1873, that he found it necessary to provide better accommodation for his numerous customers, and built a large clubroom at the side.

Although this backfired somewhat, for later in 1877, he was forced to close the Inn to all indoor drinking on Sundays, probably due the general temperance movement at that time, against drinking on a Sunday, but opened 2 hours to sell beer to be taken home, from 12 30pm to 1 30pm, and from 7pm to 8pm, in the evening. The change met with the approval of Nunneley & Eady, of Mkt. Harborough, also the owners of two other public houses in the village, and all new tenants of theirs had to comply with similar rules on entering one of their houses.

Later in August 1926, plans were passed to build the new Porch and Bay Windows on the front of the Inn, owned at the time by Eddy & Dulley, "The Brewery", at Mkt. Harborough.

A drawing by Miss Jean Coleman of the Old Swan in 1962, the Inn owned at that time by Phipps Northampton Brewery.

Your curiosity would then have taken you to the top of Weir Road, the last of the road names the council changed in 1900, from Weir Lane.

F. A. Boniface, in 1903, shortly after he and his children founded the well-known company. With Frederick in front, and Daisy Boniface standing to the rear of Kitty, the white pony. On the carriages are, Ruby, Frederick Percy, Leonard Arthur and Ethel Vivian Boniface, then Tom Shave, (who, later with his wife Florence were the Innkeepers at the Foxhound from c 1928, until it closed), then Cecil John (Jack) Porter, and the last two unknown.

On seeing F. A. Boniface's livery and posting stables, your family, friends, and growing number of followers, decide to treat themselves to the return journey, and arrange for all their horse-drawn carriages to meet you at the end of the Harcourt section of our tour a couple of hours later.

Weir Rd. 1903.

The house to the left of the livery stables, with *Beatrice and Evelyn Bromley in the doorway, was, until around 1890 – another of Kibworth's extinct Inns, its name long gone in the mist of time.*

Next to this, the houses no longer there, while further down in Barrack's Yard, twelve cottages once stood, with one of these also a shop, but by 1934, most of these were in such a poor condition that a clearance order was made and all but one were demolished in 1936, the tenants housed in other parts of the village.

While opposite, the first house in the road was the old thatched cottage, belonging to the Bromley family (currently being restored in 2004). Next to these, one of the many cottages owned by G Lynn, this pair he utilised as a storehouse for his supplies, while further down stands the three story houses and the attached cottages, parts of which were a glove factory until the 1860s.

In the distance, the fields and weir, known as the "Floodies", where the parish council often used the service of the Town Crier for inviting tenders for the upkeep of the Wash pit there.

As we turn and stroll into "Pinfold Lane"[2] – its ancient name from the time it was a bridle-way that ran from the east, down Weir lane and to the west of the village, your assemblage all wonder why on earth they abandoned its name entirely – into the mind-boggling new name it probably acquired by default, when the bridle-way was improved around 1800, shortly before the new section of the turnpike was constructed in 1810.

Anyway, we pause just beyond the corner of the new road, at the location where the village stocks once stood, and although they had not been used legally since 1834, they remained there until January 1860, when some "Rebeccaites" thinking them of little use, pulled them up and laid them in the streets.

Of the "Pinfold" itself, where the stray cattle were retained before the fields were enclosed until re-claimed by their owners, was probably sixty odd yards further down and near the end of the lane, the remainder of the road as we know it today still un-made.

While opposite – at the time of our tour, the Old Swan, and the thatched cottage to its right – owned by Mr Mason, were the only buildings in the road, apart from those belonging to the Gas Co.

Glancing down New Rd. we contemplate on the location where Kibworth Town Football Club first played until 1900. For the first three years after the club was formed for the 1893-4 season, they played some way from the centre of the village, and sadly lost in the fog of ones memory, but they, and their reserves played in the Mkt. Harborough League.

By the start of the 1896 season the Club had 59 members. The first team played in the Leicester league and had also moved to a field occupied by Mr. Mason on the New Rd, and the local reporter states they kick off either up, or down the slope. The gate money proved far more successful than was expected after having moved to the new ground, with 1132 having paid for admission to the first teams matches and 200 to the reserves, and they raised the "gate" to 2d for first team matches. That season though was a poor one for the club – in one match against Belvior St. Michael they returned defeated 14 – 0, and at the end of the season, having played 22; won 2; lost 15; drew 5, with 29 goals for, and 92 against, they finished with 9 points and bottom of the league.

The field on New Rd., was one of the larger ones, because the following year they purchased some goal nets, and also some rope to surround the playing area from the cattle that grazed there, this though left them short of money and they had to stop paying the players travelling expenses. But by the start of the 1899 season, they are back in the Harborough league, and had secured Mr Mason's field again – where it again states the pitch was on a slope. *It is believed this is the field opposite the Gas works in the following photograph, the then open field on the right of the road.*

As well as the Town, the Grammar School also had a football team, combining both teachers and the elder pupils.

The village also had another football team who also played from 1894, under the splendid name of the "Kibworth Excelsior's", and who were still in existence at the time of our tour, but the location where they played is uncertain.

Candle Power v. Gas

In 1792, William Murdock, a British engineer, lighted his home with gas he made from coal; ten years later he then lighted the outside of a factory with gaslight. By 1804 he had installed 900 gaslights in cotton mills, and became known as the father of the gas industry. His work and others – interested Frederick Albert Winsor, a German businessman. Winsor decided to manufacture gas on a large scale – learned the process from Murdock and obtained a British patent for manufacturing gas in 1804. In 1807, Winsor and his partners staged the first public street lighting with gas along Pall Mall, in London. They formed the first gas company in 1812.

The Gas Works from the open fields, now Links Rd.

Some forty or so years later – in the years following those, many attempts were made to introduce gas into the village, but the movers, subjected to pressure from the "we don't want brigade in the village" – gave in, but eventually Mr. T. Macaulay Esq., and Mr. J. Loveday, came along, neither of whom would be intimidated and both determined to fight to the end, and nearly 40 ratepayers attended a vestry meeting on Monday 20 January 1862, but with the large numbers the meeting adjourned to the school-room.

They heard of the expense that would fall upon the ratepayers by the introduction of the gas works, one obstacle being the value of the land required. A survey had been carried out in the village and fifty-three ratepayers had promised to take 220 private lights and the railway company 18, so that with 20 lights for the streets, they would have nearly 300 lights to commence with. The amount raised upon house property was 3d, and land at 1d in the pound, it was only a question of time before gas would ultimately be introduced to the village. The ten lamps at each village would cost no more than £25 per year, but as with other meetings in Kibworth's past a very long, angry, and desultory discussion ensued (and probably still do), until the Rev. F. Islip said those who did not want gas themselves ought not to hinder those who did want it – let the company be formed – the pipes laid, and then determine whether the streets should be lighted.

The parties split into two groups, and one of several non-resident occupiers of large farms, who had been specially imported by those in the village against progress – to vote against the gas, became convinced and voted with the "light side", but he was laid hold of by the "darkies" who attempted to pull him to their side, he refused to, and a vote was taken – but because of the confusion as to who was entitled to vote and who wasn't, the "light side" demanded a poll of the ratepayers of the parish according to the Act. The churchwardens at first refused this, but the storm became so boisterous that in the end they allowed it, which – when it was held – went the way of the "light side".

So in April a company was formed and by June the tender for the new Gas Works at Kibworth was accepted, but after all the effort the streets were left in darkness, the company only laying down pipes to supply private lights.

By November the Gas Works was complete, the Railway Station, Chapel and many private houses already lighted, and on Friday evening the 28th a dinner was held at the Rose & Crown, to celebrate the opening of the Gas Works, and by the time of their first AGM on the 18 May 1863, they had received powers to extend the works to Smeeton, and work was due to start to lay the one mile of piping required.

Previously in March, at vestry meeting they decide to light St. Wilfreds Church by Gas, and in feast week – following the custom of past years, a special service was held on Wednesday evening the 28th October in commemoration of the dedication of the church, when the lights were used for the first time, and in Beauchamp the streets were lighted for the first time in the winter of 1863.

In September 1864 the village attempted to adopt the Lighting & Watching Act, so the street could be lighted and paid for by all the ratepayers. Though proposed at first, it was abandoned as many landowners and occupiers objected to them being rated for the purpose, but in Beauchamp the streets were lighted again with some difficulty by private subscription.

The following year there were 26 lamps in the two parishes and the cost of lighting them was 25 shillings each, as the amount was unlikely to be collected they request the church-wardens convene a meeting, to pass a motion for the rating of house property in Beauchamp, and that a rate of £20 was not to be exceeded. At a later meeting this was reduced to £17 10s for lighting the streets for the coming winter, but in Harcourt it was not until 1870 when they light the streets again.

By August 1871 the demand for gas had increased to such an extent that the Gas Co., decide to build a new and large gas tank 41' 6" in diameter by 14' deep. The same year in Beauchamp the street lamps were again lit, when several gentlemen undertook the collection as well as the payment, but in Harcourt difficulty still prevailed in getting the inhabitants to subscribe the sum to pay for the streetlights, so because they had not fully adopted the Act making it compulsory, the street remained unlit.

The local papers of the time did seem to have it in for the residents of Harcourt, and not only on the subject of the gas, for a reporter wrote: "The Kibworth Gas Co., have made known their intention of removing those adornments from the streets of Kibworth Harcourt in consequence of the inhabitants preferring the village to remain in a state of darkness, to subscribing the paltry sum necessary for its illumination. That this proceeding should be necessary in the present age of progression and general acceleration is certainly no small stigma on the residents of this aristocratic and so-called enlightened village."

The same problem was still evident the following November – when he wrote: "The inhabitants of Kibworth Beauchamp often laugh and chaff those of Kibworth Harcourt, or more properly speaking those of "dark" Kibworth, as it is now very familiarly called, because they cannot, or will not raise the £15., which is all that is required to light the few street lamps in that part of the village. At the last AGM of the Gas Co., we believe a resolution was passed giving the directors the powers to remove the whole of the lamps posts and brackets in Harcourt, if the lamps were not lighted by Christmas. Whether they are to be removed remains to be seen, but at present there appears but a small chance of their being lighted. A gentleman, who no doubt knows the cause of darkness, has written to the directors to know if they will not light the lamps and the answer is, they are prepared to do so – provided the said gentleman will guarantee the money. The money guarantee has not so far been given. No one this year will attempt the voluntary principle to try to raise the money as it had been so often tried and found wanting."

Twelve months later in 1873, after the threat "this resulted to there being once more illuminated. After a total eclipse extending over two winters it is not remarkable that the inhabitants should now appreciate and enjoy the return of a light which people in their right mind would never have submitted to have done without."

This though, was not to last, so in October 1874 the voluntary principle again having failed to light the streets of Kibworth, at a meeting of all ratepayers at the village hall they decided to adopt the Lighting & Watching Act., carried unanimously at a later vestry meeting. The Inspector was appointed at a rate of £30, for the year, he at once commenced business and the streets were again lighted.

The first lamplighter's name is not mentioned until 1894, when they re-appoint Mr. Green as the Lamplighter, on a salary of 7/- per week. Two years later he asked – and was instructed to light them when necessary irrespective of the moon, his task was to light each individual lamp at dusk, then return at 10.00pm to turn them off.

Things were about to improve though with the introduction of the Parish and Local Government Act of Parliament in 1894, which generally followed the ecclesiastical parish boundaries, when the duties of the vestry were taken over by the Parish Council. At the time there were about 13600 Parishes in England.

The first meeting of the newly elected Kibworth Harcourt Parish Council, took place on the evening of Friday 14 December 1894.

The first meeting of Kibworth Beauchamp Parish Council was held on January 3rd 1895 at the Nation Schoolroom.

In 1897 after many discussions they decide to erect a lamp in the centre of the

Bank, with stone base, pedestal and three-branch light" and the following February – they accept the Jubilee Committee's offer for a Jubilee Memorial Lamp. They decide to move the present King lamp to a position near the Coach & Horses Inn. Later in June the Gas Co., decide to re-lay the gas pipes in Kibworth and to Smeeton.

Meanwhile at Smeeton in August 1901, 39 years after the Gas Co. installed the pipes; the villagers were told at a meeting in the schoolroom that if any streets required lighting they were those of Smeeton, and people wondered why there were not more accidents on the winding roads. Ten standard, two brackets and one arch bracket at the school would suffice, with an outlay of £42. The cost of lighting each lamp was estimated at about 14s per year, and 5s per week to the lamplighter, a total of £16 a year. A $^3/_4$d rate on land and $2^1/_4$d, on houses would yield about £15; they did not think any landlord would raise the rents for so trifling an outlay. A £5 a year cottage would only cost 1s a year extra, having the streets lighted. Each of the standards would cost about £3. 15s and two gentlemen had promised to provide one each and erect them as parish property.

In the end after a vote, 14 were in favour of lighting and 6 against thus securing the required two-thirds, but then – a poll of the village was demanded, which took place on Wednesday 28th August, and resulted in the defeat of the proposition for lighting the streets. At the time there were 92 voters registered, 34 votes were in favour and 30 against, and as a two-thirds majority of the voting members was required for the adoption of the Act, the scheme failed. However – through the enterprise of a few of the more progressive sprits in the village – lamp-posts were nevertheless erected and the streets were lighted by gas in the winter of 1901, and in order that the entire length of road between Kibworth and Smeeton be illuminated, the parish council of the latter erected extra lamps to meet those of their neighbours.

The street lamps were lighted in the village in 1902, as a reminder to King Edward's Coronation, the cost of the gas being met by private subscription. However, by 1903 owing to the cost – the Smeeton streets, as well as the road extending to the Kibworth boundary were in darkness again, with every prospect of remaining so, the gloom upsetting many of the residents with the glow from the Kibworth lights.

The standards remained intact, but no lights had been seen since 1905, or would be – until later on Friday 27 October 1922, when – at a meeting of parishioners at the school hall to consider the advisability of again lighting the streets, and a show of hands resulted in 18 for, and 10 against putting the Street Lighting Act in force in the village. In further discussions, lively words ensued, but on a vote 20 were for, and 8 against lighting the village, so the council saw that the lamps were again lighted.

While back at Kibworth, in November 1902, KBPC decide to place lights in Dover St. and Gladstone St., at once, and a year later the lamplighter's salary was increased to 11/- a week

It was not until 1913, that the Lighting Committee made arrangements to purchase 45 Automatic Lights for the street lamps at 18/- each.

During the First World War the streetlights remained unlit, but by January 1918 they decide that 17 lamps are to be lighted again until 9.30pm, with special arrangements to be made with the special constables in case of an Air Raid, and by 1919 all were lit again until 10.00pm

In 1927, the Leicestershire & Warwickshire Electric Power Co. (L&WEP Co.,) apply to install power lines etc. to the village, but is was not until August 1930, that the scheme for electric lighting of the public streets was adopted. In October, Beauchamp decide the lighting of the centre lamp on the Bank should be by electric. They then decide to remove all the existing Gas Lamps, Heads & Clocks and store them in Dr. Macbeth's stables (22 – 24 High St.), at a rent of 2/6 per week, and to offer them for sale, although who they thought would buy them when everywhere else had been converted by then is anyone's guess, but then along comes good old Harcourt – who purchase some for £20, and they advertise the Gas Standards at £3-10-0 each. Later they sell four more to Harcourt for £10.

Later in 1933, an application from tenants at Kibworth to the Rural District Council for electric lights to be put in, but they decide that tenants already with gas, must bear the cost themselves, and the following year the parish council were asked to light the Turnpike.

At times though, the L&WEP Co. were fairly generous, and from 1935 they state they were willing to keep the streets lamps alight all night during Christmas week, December 23rd to the 27th, free of cost, which the parish council accepted.

In 1937 they place two new lamps in Halford St. and Imperial St. [Ave.], and to erect a lamp post in Little End. The following year they instruct the Gas Co. to remove the old lamp post facing the Coach & Horses Inn, and two years later the remaining gas lamp posts were removed.

In April 1943, the Jubilee Lamp was blown down during a gale, but they decide not to repair it until after the War. Then in March 1944 they hear it will cost £100 to repair, and later in 1945, plans were submitted to replace the one blown down, but it was not until April 1948 that they accept plans for the new light, and take preliminary steps to erect the same, and in October 1949, they ask Leicestershire County Council for permission to borrow £250 to cover the purchase and erection of the new lamps in the Village, and erection (1950/1) of the central lamp in the square.

New Road to the Railway Station

Resuming our tour, and looking past the gas works to the railway bridge, which, if the Midland Railway Co., had constructed the railway on the original planned course of their line in 1846, the bridge would not be there at all, but would have crossed the turnpike, further north, about 75 yards on the Leicester side of New Road.

New Road Bridge, c 1910.

As a passenger train pulled by a Johnson Class 2-4-0 heads for Leicester, your attention is drawn to the original height of the parapets, this bridge and the one over the turnpike to Harborough, would be replaced later in 1915 after 60 years service with another steel bridge, and the height of the parapets raised, with the top half of each side further away from the line.

We then turn and head back to the "Bank", on arriving there, a disgruntled spectator who had left the cricket field, remarked that five of the home team had now managed the magnificent feat of being dismissed for a "duck".

Turning right and head towards the station, and facing you now is 9 Station St., with its white painted walls – the shop owned by John Hind; painter, the building that would become Beauchamp's fourth Sub-Post Office from c 1945, prior to its re-location to 40 High St. around 1977, beyond that the sign for J. Mason, builder in his garden – whose family built the Villas, then next to the garden, Ingram's, the tailor.

Next to which stands Kibworth and Smeeton's Village Hall, built after the rector had purchased the ground for the hall. It was built in April 1866, after a joint stock company was formed, with a capital of £500, with shares at £5.00 each to ensure its erection. After it opened it became the location for Kibworth's Reading Room, and many Penny Readings and concerts were held there, to raise the funds

A second or third generation faded photograph, which accounts for its poor
condition, the original of which sadly went "missing" while out on loan around
40 years ago, but it is one of the earliest of Station St., in the 1890s.

for that and other good causes in the villages.

For many years prior to the opening of the village hall, it had been the custom
at Kibworth, for the wives of the labourers and others to solicit alms – called
"Gooding", the practice of begging. At one time it was confined to old women and
widows, but of late years, as soon as a girl married – she went "St. Thomasing", on
St Thomas's Day, the 21st December and the shortest day of the year. In 1878
however, the practice stopped, when several ladies apparently tired of the annual
knocking on their doors, raised the subscriptions to provide tea at the village hall,
to which all above a certain age were invited. After tea the widows were presented
with two ounces of tea, and the others a quarter of a pound each, and 1s.

Later in December 1916 the village hall was also from where – after a canvass
of the village, over £120 was subscribed by the villagers in less than a week to provide the necessary funds to send Christmas gifts to Kibworth's Soldiers and Sailors.
Over 200 parcels were sent – each costing, including postage, an average of 12s 9d.,
and every parcel contained 100 cigarettes, 2oz. tobacco, 1 tin malted milk, 1 tablet
of soap, 1 tin of Vaseline, 1 tin Oxo tablets, 1 tin peppermints, $^{1}/_{2}$lb. chocolate, 1
handkerchief, 1 wool scarf, 1 writing pad, 1 Christmas card, and 1 hussiff (army
slang for a "housewife" a packet containing cotton, needles, pins, etc.)

Next to the hall, at number 17 Station St., from around 1908 was to become
Beauchamp's third post office, with Charles W. Cooper moving from the
"Harcourt" office.

Beyond that – "Beauchamp Cottages", also built by the Mason family, where
at number 23, the "National Telephone Co. Ltd.", had recently (1906[6]) opened
their call office, with Mrs. A. Grant the operator, but as there would be a shortage
of lines at first, most of them would be shared, with the numbering system of: 1,
1X, 1Y, 2, 2X, 2Y, 3, etc. With No. 1; G. Murray Smith, Gumley Hall, Gumley, 1Y;
E. V. Phillips, Doctor, 2; R. J. Poynor, Hosiery Manufacture, 2Y; Boniface & Co.,

Hack Masters, Weir Rd., 3; Edward Mason, Builder, 3Y; George Lynn Ltd., Grocer, 4; The Railway Arms, 5; Johnson & Barnes, Hosiery Manufacturer, 6; Midland Railway Co., amongst them, and with 18; the "National Telephone Co. Ltd.", and 50; H. Moss, Plumber, also being public call offices.

While nearly opposite that, the original Railway Arms owned by the Lichfield Brewery Co. At one time – until around 1885, in the far end of their yard at the rear – stood the Reformed Methodists Chapel, known as the "Little Chapel", which closed due to the lack of a congregation.

The "Railway Arms", c 1905.

Then next to the Inn – the three cottages, finally demolished in 1926 along with the original Inn.

The "Railway Arms", c 1905.

At the rear of the Inn, Frederick Boniface kept more of his horses and carriages, as well as the shoeing forge in the far right hand corner of the yard, run by Percy French.

When Frederick's son Leonard kept the Inn (from c 1912-1937), the Lichfield Brewery Co. (Ind Coope), first drew up the original plans to demolish the Inn and the cottages next door in 1921, but this and the re-building of the Inn did not take place until March 1926, with the Inn sign on the later plans showing that they proposed to re-name the Inn as the "Railway Hotel", and which it is believed to have remained so for around 10 years. To keep the licence open – the skittle ally was used as the Inn for the period of its re-building, and the family living at 35 Church Rd.

Next to the Inn and the jitty, Alonzo Freeland's Chemist shop. Then the tin hut, occupied by the "Kibworth Mineral & Aerated Water Manufactory", and later where Tommy Hawkins's motor repair business was situated.

The Coming and Going
of the Station

After which a short distance down the approach to the station – the large goods sheds, built approximately where the first rectory once stood.

The Station Approach, c 1930, the smoke from a train passing through the station.

Further on the buildings used by the local coal merchants, and in front of those – the weighbridge. We then venture into the station where our group then split and sit on the two seats on each platform, and at the same time refresh ourselves with several jugs of best brew supplied by Edward Peberdy, who had been the Innkeeper at the Railway Arms for the past 18 years, while we reflect chronologically on the coming and going of the railway.

The railway through Kibworth, came into being when three companies; the "Midland Counties", opened 30 May 1839; the "Birmingham & Derby Junction Railway", opened 2 August 1839, and the "North Midland Railway Co.", opened on 11 May 1840, came together to form the "Midland Railway Co.", on 10 May 1844.[3]

From the start in 1845, when the proposed line was first surveyed prior to the prospectus being published, they met with opposition in every field, due to the irresponsible way the survey was conducted, with some of the officials refusing to give their names and the line they represented, and even in the presence of the occupiers, levelled crops and hedges to the ground, annoying the tenants and local landowners, who were determined to offer every opposition, so a strong police force was in readiness in case of need.

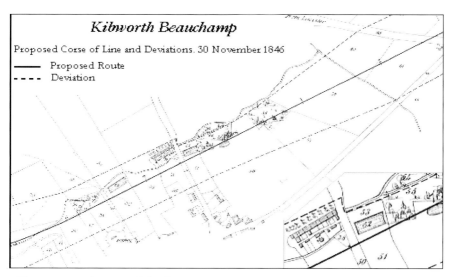

The proposed route of the line through Kibworth, the eventual course of the line was near its southern-most deviation.

However, the Midland slumped to near-bankruptcy after a great upheaval, initially caused by George Stephenson's death at Chesterfield on the 12 August 1848. This continued when George Hudson, who at one point in his career controlled more than 990 route miles of railway, but in the mid-1840s, he bought two railways that were losing money. Soon all his railways were in trouble and he resigned over allegations that he had "manipulated" various company accounts, he went bankrupt in 1848.

John Ellis, the new chairman changed its fortunes and by 1851 a new wave of optimism was experienced in railway circles. The scheme for constructing the Leicester to Hitchen line was revived – which had replaced an earlier South

Midland Railway scheme by the Midland, originally raised by an 1847 Act, but relinquished in July 1850, then rescued by the Leicester to Bedford party. The Leicester & Hitchen Railway received Royal Assent on the 4 August 1853.

In March 1854, at the Midland Railway's 20th half yearly general meeting held at the Derby Station, chairman said: "With respect to the Leicester to Hitchen line, he still entertained as high an opinion of its necessity as ever he did; and he was happy to say that the neighbouring landowners had met them in the most cordial and liberal sprit (No doubt forgetting the problems nine years previous). Their engineer, too, had revised his estimate of the cost of the construction of the line, and there would be no large stations to construct, and, allowing for engineering and law expenses, there would be a margin of £50,000 within the £1,000,000 first estimated; and if, as he believed this could be done, he predicted this would be the cheapest and most profitable £1,000,000 they had ever expended."

By July, construction at Kibworth was under way, and on Sundays large numbers of the inhabitants went along the line to see how the work has progressed during the week. This didn't go down too well with the local preachers with the loss of their congregation, and on a Sunday evening a Wesleyan local preacher endeavoured to arrest the attention of the people by preaching in the "gully hole." The following Sunday the minister of the Independent Chapel preached at the same place, instead of his own chapel.

In August, the first fatal accident occurred on the railway here, the deceased – a driver, had only been at work for half a hour on his first day, and as he returned from the "gully hole" with a set of full wagons, about 20 tons of earth which had been undermined and the pegs removed for the purpose of displacing it – fell on him – crushing him against one of the wagons. He was interred near Michael Ingo, killed by the upheaval of the express stagecoach as it passed through Kibworth 20 years previously.

By February 1855, about three-quarter of the embankment had been made up to where the lines crosses the turnpike, but the work there had come to a standstill, waiting for the girders for the bridge across the road, the men there were at work constructing the roads for the field bridges. The girders were erected in June, and in September, they decide that the Kibworth station, is to be erected in a small field belonging to the Rectory.

Church Hill, had been partly taken down by April 1856, to make the embankment and a better approach to the station from the North, and all that remained was the brickwork for turning the arches to the station bridge, but the following Autumn – heavy rain caused the approach to the bridge over the railway to give way in many places, and required repairing during the winter.

With the rapid progress of the railway there was increasing excitement in the village, the permanent rails were already laid, and the first engine came through Kibworth on Wednesday evening the 2 July 1856, when at least 200 people assembled to see it – many of whom had never seen a railway engine before. It stopped for a short time to deliver material and two of the trucks rapidly filled with people – who were eager to say they had rode in the first train through Kibworth, but as they were proceeding to the ballast hole near Glen, they ran into some earth wagons on the line, no damage was done by this first collision, besides knocking several wagons off the line.

By October, the railway from the junctions at Wigston and Harborough was nearly complete; the whole was ballasted and ready for traffic. The building of Kibworth station was progressing rapidly and the signal box was complete, with work about to start on the station yard.

The engine which was used for ballasting on the line was involved in an accident while returning to Leicester, and as it approached Newton Harcourt, it ran into a number of wagons that had been left on the line, breaking two into pieces, threw others off the line and disabling them. The stoker was slightly hurt; there were a number of workmen in a wagon behind the engine, returning home after the days work, they were all thrown into a heap. Had they been in the wagon in front of the engine, as they frequently were, some lives would have been sacrificed. It appears a Kibworth man should have warned the driver of the obstruction before leaving Kibworth, but had neglected to do so.

By February 1857, the earthwork was complete and a track formed through all the cuttings, the bridgework nearly completed, and little was to be done except finishing coupling, etc., of the permanent way.

The brickwork of the station was nearly complete, most of the buildings roofed in and the offices ready. On April 14th the employees were placed at the various stations and posts along the line, and on Wednesday the 15th coals etc., were brought up, then on the 2nd May, the Government Inspectors passed over the line, testing the bridges and otherwise inspecting it, so that it could shortly be opened for passengers.

In the construction of the section of the railway through Kibworth, as well as the one reported fatality, there were a further nine accidents on this stretch alone, many resulting in broken bones and at least one amputation – of a leg.

It is now time to ponder – not on documented facts still available – but on information from previous Kibworthians – handed down through the generations, when in 2003 – Roger said: – that his grandfather said – that he was told by Arthur – whose grandfather (or was it his great grandfather? – Maybe – phew! – well anyway) – who was a signal-man in the first signal box on Kibworth Station – said: that at one stage there was a manned level crossing complete with gates – near the station.

There isn't any record of this, as most of the early records and plans of the Midland railway no longer exist. *I can only guess that when they were lowering Church Hill and moving the soil to build the Station Bridge access for carts and pedestrians alike, would have been extremely difficult, and it is possible that for a year, when the line was already in place, and prior to the completion of the bridge, and the opening of the railway, a separate crossing was made as a temporary measure to allow access between the two villages, probably on the Harborough side of the bridge, and access to the crossing probably down where the present path to the allotment are, across the line and up the station approach.*

The crossing was probably covered later when the platforms were extended. The first Signal Box used to stand on the bridge end of the Leicester platform, but was re-sited at the southern end of the south (Harborough) platform around that time. That was replaced in 1889, and the old signal box was moved at the time by Robert Holt, carpenter (when he was told of the above by Arthur's grandfather), for – and into the garden of the Rev Fawssett at Smeeton to use as a summerhouse, which remained there until the late 1980s.

The Midland Railway Co., opened on the 15 April 1857 for goods traffic, and the formal opening of the line by the Directors was on Thursday 7th May, when trains were put on, calling at all the intermediate stations between Leicester and Hitchen, and for passengers on 8 May 1857.

The opening caused a very large number of people to assemble at the Harborough Station to witness the trains pass, a special trip to Leicester was laid on – but most preferred a cheap one to Bedford. At Kibworth hundreds of people assembled on the bridge near the station and along the line to cheer the trains as they passed. In the evening and the following day, the "navvies" went around the village collecting subscriptions from the inhabitants for a holiday. The sad part on the coming – was the going, for the last of the Stage Coaches between Harborough and Leicester ceased running on the Saturday prior to the opening of the railway. Their first timetable gives the trains stopping at Kibworth from Leicester as: 6.27am., 8.32am, 1.27pm and 6.07pm., on weekdays and 8.02am and 6.32pm on Sundays. From Harborough to Leicester at 8.31am, 11.09am 1.34pm, and 8.34p.m. and at 10.34am and 8.31pm on Sundays. The travelling time on the up line to Harborough was 18 minutes, and the down line to Leicester – 29 minutes, and 33 minutes if they stopped at Glenn and Wigston.

A report on the Mkt. Harborough Petty Sessions, held on 10 April 1860, states: "The Rev Hildebrand, Headmaster of Grammar School (1836-70), summoned the Directors of the Midland Railway Co., to show cause why they refused to build a bridge across the line at Kibworth, on land which he owned privately, through which the railway passed through centre of, and a level crossing was made, but he required a bridge. The general Act gave power to come and make applications for one if necessity exists for it, within five years. As being within time he contended he was right. The Midland Railway Co. stated that he was not in time and that five years had elapsed from the passing of the Act, and was not entitled to ask for a bridge instead of a the level crossing he had. The Magistrate did not allow it, but after further submissions they asked the Magistrate to visit the site, so that better evidences may be brought before him. He agreed and case adjourned for one month."

There is no mention of the case at the following sessions reported in the papers, and the actual minutes for the case no longer exist, nor is there any mention of this in the Grammar School minutes, it does though state that he had private land of his own, but not where. *This, according to senior Kibworthians, is believed to refer to the School Lane level crossing and the bridge was built shortly after the case was settled out of court.*

The platforms were extended in 1862 and again in 1870, and in July 1871 the directors of the Midland Railway Co., granted the request of Mr. J. Underwood, and other inhabitants of the village, by placing four handsome iron seats on the platforms at the station – the seats your party are now sitting on.

Leicester platform and seats, c 1910.

In February 1872 they commenced the working of the block signal system at Kibworth. Two new signal boxes had been put in, one at Warwick Rd. Bridge, and the other on the Harborough side of the station.

Later in April, the Way wardens considered the weak state of the station bridge embankment, and if it slipped who was responsible, they had recently widened the approach on one side by placing faggots to put the earth on, the surveyor did not consider this safe as it was sinking, and the road was ankle deep in mud that people could not cross to their houses.

During the three-year period from 1872–74, there was an average of 29,033 passengers a year carried from Kibworth.

In October 1874, the Midland Railway decided to abolish the 2nd class carriages and change the uniform rate, a 1st class ticket would now cost 11/2d per mile and 1d for 3rd class, and it would take effect from the 1 January 1875. The second-class carriages made third class, and the old wooden thirds were broken up as fast as they could be replaced. They then announced that in future all third-class carriages would have upholstered seats. The travelling public were delighted, but the innovation was greeted by other companies (who were envious of the Midland's record) with dismay and "pampering the working classes."

Their timetable, 17 years on – states the train departing Kibworth at 7.51am, arrives at Leicester at 8.12am, stopping at Great Glen and Wigston. Wow! – Can you imagine that – 21 minutes to the centre of Leicester – unbelievable!

The village had a narrow escape from a major disaster on 9 October 1880, when only two persons were injured when the Midland Scotch Express crashed on a foggy night, north of the station, and according to the reports of the near disaster in the national papers at the time – Kibworth had gained a tunnel !

In fact the train had left St. Pancras, and while passing Kibworth Station the driver suspected something had gone wrong with the driving gear of the engine. He applied the Westinghouse vacuum brake, and pulled the train up in reverse gear, in a very deep and dark cutting, north of Kibworth Station. After examining the engine, the steam was turned on – still in reverse gear, this sent the train back at a rapid rate, and although when the mistake was discovered – the brake was applied, the train came into collision with an ironstone train which had been in the Gumley sidings waiting for the express to pass, allowed back on the main line, and was standing at the signals – just north of the station. The force of the collision was very great – the enormous pressure wrecking the weakest part of the train. The guards van bounded off the engine of the mineral train, and the momentum of the front portion of the train crushed the rearmost carriages.

Later in 1885, the wooden steps from the road bridge to each platform were built. The following year a footbridge was attached to the platform side of the road bridge wall to link the two together.

On the 1886 Ordnance Survey Map, a level crossing is shown where the "Tin Bridge is now, and the Bridge between that and the School Lane, is still complete over the railway.

Documents exists that suggest that the station bridge at first was only 14 feet wide, and in May 1892, the Highway Board decided to widen the bridge by 15 feet, 10 feet on one side and 5 feet on the other so making it 29 feet wide, at an estimated cost of £50 to £60.

The Telegraph facilities in their office at Kibworth Station, which for some years had been closed was reopened on Wednesday 26 August 1893 for the public, useful for sending messages after 8pm, the hour at which the post office closed.

Later in December 1895, plans were passed for the widening of the approach on either side of the bridge. One section starting at the station approach itself to start of the bridge, and either side of the road starting at the entrance to the allotments to about half the length of the road to the apex of the bridge.

On the 29 November 1897, at the Kibworth Beauchamp Parish Council meeting they discuss the dangerous level crossing a few hundred yards on the Glen side of the station. It was carried that: "That the Midland Railway Co., in view of the largely increased traffic over the level crossing in the Parish of Kibworth Beauchamp, owing to the springing up of a new factory along the Fleckney Road (J & B), be asked to kindly remove the danger by erecting a bridge at the spot". Later they write to them again in 1899 and finally the Midland Railway Co., respond to the application in 1900, and state that the directors, when on tour of inspection would visit the spot. As previously mentioned in August 1903 they agreed to build the bridge. Although on the 1904 map the crossing is still shown, as also is the next bridge before the School Road one, so it was probably built late in 1904.

For the serious steam railway buffs (probably all of us if the truth is known) – the chronology of Kibworth's Signal Boxes and Slow Lane from 1889 are:

Kibworth's Signal Box's: The station box was re-placed and opened on 4-3-1889. Later Re-framed 20-9-1914. It was replaced on 17-10-1926. Burnt out and restored on 8-1-1984. It closed on 29-6-1986.

Kibworth Station to North Box: Down Slow Line. Opened 7-12-1926, made Down Slow Line on 17-11-1929, and made loop 28-4-1969.

Kibworth North Box replacement opened 25-1-1903, 2nd replacement opened 3-1-1926. It closed 28-4-1968.

Kibworth North to Wistow: Up Goods Line. It opened 16-1-1927. The down goods line was opened 17-11-1929.[4]

In 1905, the wooden steps over the bridge at the station were moved further

The original pedestrian bridge to cross over the line around 1905, situated on the station side of the road bridge.

Station Bridge later in c 1950.

apart to give a wider access through to the foot crossing on the Leicester side of the road bridge.

The start of the sidings that ran to the end of the Villas can be seen beyond the bridge on both photographs. At first they were used to load the gravel from the nearby pits, then later the cattle docks were situated there. At some stage later, the timber bridge was removed and two gates were installed at the top of the steps, to allow the public to cross the line on the roadside pavement.

During the three-year period from 1920–22, the average passengers carried had increased to 41,014, with 124 weekly train departures from Kibworth.

In 1923, the Midland Railway Co. became the London Midland & Scottish

Railway Co.

At their meeting on 12 December 1923, KBPC view the plans dated November 1923 for the widening of the railway line from Kibworth Station to Wistow Box by the LMSR Co., they were passed at the next meeting on 2 January 1924, but by their next meeting on the 6 February, they had received a verbal application from the Midland Railway Co. in connection with the suggested widening of the track and to remove permanently, the Wooden Footbridge (at Johnny's Brook) over the Railway. They protested against this, for if it was carried out, the pedestrians would have to walk down High St., to the School Lane footpath. They reply to this effect.

The RDC receive the plans (No. 77) for the widening of Wistow Rd. Bridge, No. 15 for two additional spans, one on each side of existing bridge.

Then on 8 August 1925, they receive the plans for new footbridge, No. 16b, "Tin Bridge" to be built about 4 yards on the Leicester side of the existing wooden bridge, and bridge No. 17 to be demolished. In November the plans were passed, and the old timber bridge demolished, as was the next bridge nearer the station, both necessary for the widening for the slow track to be laid. So the new Tin Bridge was built by the time the slow line opened in November 1926, and all that remains of the next bridge nearer the station is a brick buttress, on the North side to support the embankment.

On 1 January 1948 the London Midland & Scottish Railway Co. and the remaining private railways became British Railways.

And finally – exactly 20 years later, that most appalling deed in the history of the railways, a slightly blurred photo of the actual notice on Kibworth Station for the closure of the station on 1 January 1968.

BRITISH RAILWAYS BOARD

LONDON MIDLAND REGION

PUBLIC NOTICE   TRANSPORT ACT, 1962

Modification of
Railway Passenger Services

LEICESTER – WELLINGBOROUGH

Following the consent of the Minister of Transport, the local train services will be modified and the following Passenger Stations will be CLOSED on and from 1st January 1968 subject to the granting by the Traffic Commissioners of licences to operate additional and revised bus services :—

DESBOROUGH & ROTHWELL   KIBWORTH

EAST LANGTON   WIGSTON MAGNA

For further information please contact your local station or :—

R. D. Gardiner,
Divisional Manager,
Furlong House,
Middle Furlong Road,
Nottingham.

The Station to Carlton Road

We continue our stroll over the station bridge – where the parapets on either side of the bridge are now a great deal safer for the public, after they were raised in 1875 – from their original height of only 3 feet, after frequent complaints of horses being frightened when passing over the bridge, by the steam and smoke from the engines below.

A photograph of an engraving, from John Nichols
History and Antiquities of the County of Leicester, printed in 1790.

While there – imagine the scene in the late eighteenth century, across the fields to St Wilfred's complete with spire, and the second rectory – it built in 1788 and demolished in 1965.

Then as we glance down "Little End" – its name at the time of our tour , or "Duck Paddler" its name prior to the coming of the railway, and where, if the Railway Co. had carried out their original plans, the line would have been closer to the houses there – than it is today, and think how much easier it would have been for the residents living there, when they would stroll out of their street while admiring the unbroken easterly view, straight onto Church Hill – near to where the brook emerges, afterwards – feeling peeved, not only with the loss of their view, but having to cope with the steep climb to exit their road.

On the opposite side of Church Hill, and back in time, stood Kibworth's first rectory (in the period covered by our tour, and probably the H-shaped building shown on the Enclosure map), and of the rectory itself, we are informed that:[7]

The Terrier of Glebe land they held in 1694, long before the fields were enclosed is also stated, with roods; half-acres; and acres of land in parts of the open-fields – known by such names as: Suffer Long Furlong; Broad Hurst; Low Little Hill; High Little Hill; Kingstock Bridge Furlong; Mill Gutter Furlong; Mill Furlong; and Stubstons Headland amongst them.[7]

In a later un-dated document, but it is probably from around the 1730s, it states:[8]

With parts of land in Mill Gutter; Mill Furlong; Warwick Back; Killpack Hole; Neather Furlong; Gallow Meere – all in Beauchamp, with Church Hill; Broad Green; Buttlings Close at Smeeton, and Ranglands and Ragward Hill in Harcourt, amongst them.[8]

Later the buildings "are thought to have been a timber framed building, and demolished because of its dilapidated state shortly after the second rectory was built in 1788. Kibworth's Tithe Barn was also in the grounds of the old rectory, and consisted of 11 bays and stables, the barn was demolished around 1788."[9] The ponds were filled in later – when the railway was constructed.

Other ancient field names that have survived on documents dated from before the enclosure act, and not owned by the glebe, include such splendid names of land south of Tur Langton Rd: Mill Furlong; Church Sick Furlong; Harborough Way Furlong; Hern Sick Furlong, and on the north of the road: Woman's Dam Furlong; Watery Hoe; Whittle Hedge Furlong, and Coomb Furlong. With to the west of Carlton Rd: Stone Hill Furlong; Crow Thorne Furlong; Furlong under Mill Hill; Old Mill Furlong; Townsend Furlong; Doe Slade Furlong; Banwell Furlong; Peaks Moor Furlong; Long Sharp Sick Furlong; Lady Pool Furlong; and Debdale Furlong, then some unreadable names around the turnpike, and to the south of Wistow Rd: Crindle Dyke Furlong, Broadlong Furlong, and Neather Cold Acre. Today, only a few of the more obvious names which still exist – although referring to the smaller enclosed fields, can be identified with any degree of certainty.[10]

As we continue our stroll up Church Hill, behind the gas street lamp and standing back from the road, is the gateway to Rectory Field, and on its right, the start of the pathway leading down to the allotments and the probable route to the level crossing.

If you were curious enough to venture into rectory field you would see part of St. Wilfred's Church and the second rectory, and where, in 1857, the Rev Osborn allowed the newly re-formed Kibworth Cricket Club to play. Previous a club had played on and off since 1847 at least, in a field some distance out of the village, but again, its location is lost in the mist of time.

> **KIBWORTH HORTICULTURAL SOCIETY.**
>
> THE SECOND EXHIBITION for 1862 will be held, by permission of the Rev. M. F. F. Osborn, in the RECTORY GROUNDS, KIBWORTH, adjoining the Railway Station, on WEDNESDAY, September 17.
>
> Admission—From One o'clock till Three, 1s.; from Three to Five, 6d.; from Five to the Close, 3d. Children under Twelve years of age, Half-price.
>
> Arrangements have been made by the Midland Railway Company to convey First and Second Class Passengers from all Stations on the Leicester and Hitchin Line to Kibworth and back, at a Single Fare for the Double Journey, on the day of the Show.
>
> The Train leaving King's Cross Station at.. 9.20 a.m.
> will stop at Desborough.
> And the Train leaving Kibworth, at ...... 9.44 p.m.
> will stop at Glen and Wigston.
> The Train leaving Leicester, at ....1.35 p.m.
> will stop at Wigston and Glen.
>
> By Permission of Col. the Rt. Hon. the Earl Howe, the Band of
>
> THE LEICESTERSHIRE YEOMANRY CAVALRY
> will attend, under the direction of
> Mr. H. Nicholson

The above advert for the Kibworth Horticultural Show, to be held on the 17 September 1862, appeared on the same page of the local paper as the previous advert on September 6th. When I first saw it, three thoughts came to mind: The 1s entry fee seemed a bit high for those times. The second made me smile, wondering how any visitors from the south – on seeing the advert and contemplating on whether to visit the show, thought they were supposed to take advantage of the double journey at the single fare, and the third – well ! – coincidence ?

The Kibworth Horticultural Society was formed in July 1856, and their first show of the year was held at Wistow Hall, on the grounds belonging to Sir. H. Halford, Bart., MP, President of the society, and at first, the second exhibition of the year, was held at the Parochial School and playground, when the Kibworth Band played during the afternoon. Although by 1862 the by now well-known Countywide second show of the year in September was held in the rectory field. After 11 years though, the first Horticultural Society in the village was dissolved through lack of funds in March 1867.

We then continue up Church Hill – passing the Villas, built in the 1870s, and on the brow of the hill, "Rectory Cottage", *built by the Rev. Osborne (Woodford)* when he was the rector between 1851-84, for the parish clerk, which during the period of our tour – was Beauchamp's first post office until c 1900, prior to that moving further along and on the opposite of the road.

A photograph of a water colour of St. Wilfred's, by local artist James Smeeton (1781-1868) on the day the steeple fell.

Then your thoughts go back to when the church spire fell on the 23 July 1825, and who you had more sympathy with, the young girl, who – after running home to tell her parents of the disaster, and that she had just jumped over the church steeple, and was severely scolded for her efforts, or James Beresford the rector, who wrote the official report in the vestry minute book, which states: "On this day at 9 o'clock in the forenoon, the Towers and Spire of Kibworth Church, which, had long been decayed on the lower part, and especially about the South West angle of this Tower, and which had, for the last four months been under repair, fell to the ground."

An early photograph of St. Wilfred's, taken prior to August 1887, showing the brick wall.

After the spire collapsed, and due to the lack of funds, at some point a red brick wall was built on the western side of the churchyard. It would be six years at least before the tower was repaired, and 37 years in total before the church was restored to its former glory inside.

St. Wilfred's Church, pre 1903.

As we pass St. Wilfred's, and admire the wrought iron fence and gates – erected to commemorate Queen Victoria's Golden Jubilee in 1887, to match the rest that remained undamaged when the spire fell.

The Post Office.

Then on our right were three shops, one of which – although it went under the name of "Kibworth Harcourt Post Office" was Beauchamp's second post office and probably so-named, either because it was situated to the north of the Harcourt doorway to St Wilfred's, or, *at one time elder Kibworthians always claimed that the boundary between the two villages was the brook,* that starts near the "Tin Bridge" and meanders along the station hollow and eventually under New Rd.

The photograph, was probably taken on a Monday, when the post men – realising how Kibworth would grow over the years, pose, demonstrating the correct way to queue – when for some reason the office is busy, so the habit seems to be of a long standing nature and probably the reason for the queues – nowadays.

On the far right of the photograph – Mr. Charles W. Cooper, sub-postmaster and photographer, taken around 1905, but by 1908 he had moved to Beauchamp's third post office at 17 Station St. At the same time Mr. James Roe became the sub-postmaster for the Harcourt post office, followed by his wife until the office there closed around 1914. Later in 1911 Charles Cooper lived in the Timber Bungalow he had built at the bottom of the allotments on Fleckney Rd.

While looking at the above photograph, and as this book has been compiled from original documented facts and photographs mainly from old postcards, perhaps now is the time to mention the dating of postcards, although not the photographs on the front.

In 1870 the Post Office issued the first plain cards, with a pre-printed stamp on one face. In 1894 they allowed other publishers cards to be sent with a $^1/_2$p stamp. One year later, a new "court card" size was introduced, but with no room for illustrations. In 1899, a new card measuring 5.5 x 3.5 inches became the standard format. Then in 1902 the divided back came into being, with the address and message on one face, and a full size illustration on the other.

At the time of our tour the "Kibworth & Great Glen Cycle Motor Store", who made cycles to order, with terms from 8s, were situated along the row, and later it also become a motor repair shop, with another grocery shop (37) to its left.

By 1912, G. E. Manfield was a cycle maker there (31), later to be run by Mrs. E. A. Mansfield

Glancing back beyond the post office to St Wilfred's, and smile when we recall that when the annual vestry meeting was held there in April 1896, and because there had been a lot of illness in the village over the past winter, they discuss whether to supply stimulants to those in need – and if it would be better to give them Wine or Brandy.

The Coach and Horses.

Moving up to "Lester Road", as it was frequently spelt well into the twentieth century, and turning left at the Coach and Horses, which, according to F. P. Woodford, "the Whitsuntide village feast was held at the rear, where exponents would take on the local champions in the wooden floored bowling ally."

At the time of our tour though, Archibald Mattock was the Publican, and part of the stables were occupied as living quarters by a stud groom, then you notice the pump and trough in front, which Dr. Marriott had substituted with a new one in 1887.

In 1889, when Henry Woodford, was the Innkeeper, he applied for the renewal of his 7 day licence, which he held until 8 or 9 years ago, when a local resident bought the property – his object of reducing it to a 6 days, to promote temperance in the neighbourhood and hoped the other Innkeepers would follow the same course, which they didn't. He failed to regain his 7-day licence.

Later in 1891 Archibald Mattock again tried for his 7-day licence, and said it was the only public house in Kibworth with a 6-day licence and had stabling for 18 horses, but was again refused, until after 20 August 1895, when the Inn was purchased by the "All Saints Brewery Co."

Beyond the Inn, two blocks of cottages, both now long gone, then think how improved the road surface was after the Rural District Council, for the second year running in 1906, had, on the portion of the main turnpike that runs through the two parishes, treated it with a patent solution to alleviate the dust nuisance, previously the turnpike was only a track 14 feet wide, of which every yard was constructed with four loads of road metal, but over the years the mud had seeped through to the surface.

Even with that, when looking at the road, it is hard to believe that in 1811, the travelling time of the stagecoaches travelling from London to Kibworth was only $13^1/_2$ hours. By 1835 with the gradual improvement in the roads, and the coming of the railway this had been reduced to $9^1/_2$ hours, about 9 miles an hour, a journey time of just over one hour from Kibworth to Leicester, a time un-attainable in 2004, especially when the school run is in full swing.

Opposite the Coach, was "Harcourt House", the residence of Dr. Marriott, later to be demolished shortly after being sold in April 1931, the purchaser proposed at first to build 30 houses, with a new road linking the Leicester and Langton Roads.

Then glance beyond the side of the house, down the footpath leading to Carlton Rd., and the cottage at the bottom – now long gone.

Leicester Rd., c 1910.

Then the garage, where in February 1886, a Mr. Smith was granted a petroleum licence to his premises, probably the first in the village, which later in 1913 was owned by the Kibworth Motor Garage, with G. E. Manfield, the manager, and to its right, Fred Hill's saddlery.

The "Foxhound", c 1940.

On the opposite side of the turnpike from Leicester to Mkt. Harborough, by now the wonky posts and wires erected by the "The United Kingdom Electric Telegraph Co." in 1863, and behind those, at one time was Harcourt's Posting House, probably taking the business over, previously carried on at the Rose & Crown.

To their right with John George Weston the Innkeeper – stands the Foxhound. This was re-built in 1876 and leased by the All Saints Brewery Co. They ceased brewing in 1925 when the company, along with 81 licensed houses including those at Kibworth and Smeeton was acquired by Ind Coope & Co., Ltd. Later in 1954 the undertaking was transferred to Ind Coope & Allsopp Ltd[5]. They closed the Foxhound in April 1954.

Had you called at the Inn on our short tour in 1905, mine host would have been Joseph Morris Coleman, Kibworth's longest serving publican, a total of 51 years at three Inns, the Admiral Nelson 1854-57, the Coach & Horses 1857-67, and finally the Foxhound, from 1867 until he retired in June 1905.

Rose & Crown Hotel in 1925 (top) and 1930 (bottom).

The Rose & Crown Hotel, with the taxicab's waiting outside in the mid 1920s. While in the field opposite that – many years previously, Mr. Teear the Innkeeper at the time, allowed it to be used for the village feast from 1877 until 1886, for the stalls, roundabouts, and shooting galleries.

Then pause to look at the Rose & Crown, where Ernest A. White was the Publican, and also leased at the time by the All Saints Brewery Co., where in the yard at the rear you see the rest of Frederick's horses and carriages being prepared for their next customer – probably your party.

"Kibworth House"

The "Lodge"

As we continue along the new section of the turnpike which opened in 1810, and after passing the footpath leading to School Lane, stands Kibworth House, owned by the Dickinson family, and demolished in 1955, and arrive at the "Lodge", standing opposite the Leicester end of Main Street.

While strolling past the Congregation Chapel, known locally as the "Top Chapel", which opened in 1759, and finally closed c 1980, and in the field (276) on the corner of the road to Wistow, and known as Townsend Lees, Kibworth's first windmill once stood from before 1400, but long gone by 1780, and beyond that field you will notice how improved the turnpike road is, after the Waywardens created the cutting there in August 1873, thus lowering "Debdale Hill"[2] when entering Kibworth from Great Glen.

The "White House" in 1897.

Before strolling down there, your attention was drawn to the "White House", which previously was the Old Crown Inn, and it possibly closed prior to 19 June 1843, after the owner and Innkeeper Mr. Hunt, sold by auction, the whole his Household Furniture, Brewing Vessels, Copper, Well-Seasoned Barrels, Beer Machine, Screens, on the premises of the "Crown Inn", Kibworth.

But previously in April, he placed an advert for: "Old Established Inn or Public House. To be Let, and may be entered upon at Midsummer next. The "Old Crown Inn", situate at Kibworth Harcourt, with large garden adjoining, good homestead, and very extensive stabling at the back. The income was very small." Although later on 16 Sept 1843, Mr. W. Phipps applied for the licence, but the application was referred, and unfortunately the outcome is unknown.

The Old House, Kibworth.

The "Manor House", "Old House", and the Three Horse Shoes,
Main St., c 1910.

Ambling down Main Street, the Publican at the Horse Shoes is Mrs Frances E. Kimbell, and the Kimbell family had been the Innkeepers and Blacksmiths there since before 1841, and around 1855 it was known as the "Blacksmith Arms". In October 1860, Merton College, Lords of the Manor of Kibworth Harcourt, purchased the Inn, and with it being in a very dilapidated state, pulled it down to erect a new Inn. When the workman was demolishing the old Inn, one of them found eight old silver coins under the old thatch. Three bore the date of 1583, but the others bore no date that could be distinguished. The coins were eventually sent to the Treasury after quite a controversy as to who should be allowed to keep them.

On the right the "Red Lion" which closed around 1842,
decked out later in 1897.

Further down on the same side as the shoes was another of Kibworth's Inns the Red Lion, which was certainly in existence in 1790, when it is the only one mentioned by Nichols. The last known Innkeeper there was Mr. Hurst Thomas in 1841, and which probably closed shortly after, and opposite the end of the outbuilding belonging to that, stands Harcourt's village pump, which, along with the one at the Three Horse Shoes, had never been known to run dry.

"Old House", built 1678.

As we move further down the hill, Francis Woodford caught up with us once again to continue as our tour guide: "There are one or two places, or objects of interest only remaining, in place rich in historical associations. One of which is the substantial structure known as the Old House, erected in the earlier half of the 17th Century, which, however, I think, cannot be as old by at least a Century, as the farmhouse adjoining the Manor House, which from its architecture must have been erected at the end of the 15th or beginning of the 16th Centuries; outside this house close to the gateway is, or was a mounting stone, by standing on which a female was enabled to mount on to the pillion or pad placed on the horse's back, behind the saddle, and to ride to the market behind her husband – or other horseman, and coaches, carts and other vehicles being unknown owing to the bad state of the roads. The present Manor House is comparatively speaking a modern structure, being, I believe the third or fourth erected on the present site. It was in front of this house and the Old House that the weekly market was held on a large square area of land, whose edges have been clipped so often that it would, indeed, today, be difficult to find sufficient space – even for the Ancient Market Cross, which stood there less than a Century ago; dismissing altogether the idea of finding standing room for the shows, merry-go-rounds, etc., for the annual feast, which was held there even in my childhood, and from recent observations I see that the right of the "many" is still ignored by the "few," who, while purchasing a little selfish reclusion during their lives, depart and leave anything but pleasant and cherished memories behind. Two fishponds belonging to and close by the Manor indicate one of the chief pleasures indulged in – by our stay-at-home ancestors. Leading directly from the Market Place, is the road or street formerly called Hog Lane, from the fact that the Pig Market was formerly held there. The two roads at the lower end were closed by two field gates 40 years ago, at which time the brook, now enclosed by a culvert, ran across the road, with the result that the City, as it was facetiously called, was often flooded with the March adjoining. The footpath through the march formally ran straight from the Church Road direct to Carlton Road, but was diverted, further west on the present march one being erected."[1]

With that, he bade us a final farewell, but – just as he was about to move off, once more came the question, "but – when did Blondin come to Kibworth?"

Francis whispers "Look .. .., ...", wink's, and with a devilish grin at the enthusiastically waiting crowd – says, don't tell them everything, keep them guessing for a few hundred years – then wanders off.

Albert St., c 1920.

Passing into "Hog Lane" or Albert Street as it is now, admiring the cottages on the left, and wonder how many of these would still be there in a few years time, while opposite the walled garden belonging to the Manor House, and in the distance the fields, which at one time were all part of Woman's Dam Furlong.

Then the original No. 1, "The City", and where – as well as the above mud cottage, *another six mud or brick thatched cottages once stood in the narrow lane, but all that remains now, are a pair of them – still intact – further up the lane, although both now enclosed and forming parts of the internal walls within a large modern exterior,* and we think of the residents living in the City, when in a dry period before the mains supply came, they had to walk 300 yards to fetch their water from the village pump, some needing many journeys each day, for their families needs.

The origins of the "City's" name, apparently evolved from a rhyming slang word used to describe the conditions at the lower end of Hog Lane – when the Pig Market was held there hundreds of year ago, and the "leftovers" from each market were heaped around that area, these in turn were diluted from time to time when the nearby brook overflowed, flooding the lower end of the lane.

Finally, before turning left, you glance across the open-field (28), now known as "Woman's Dam" with not a house in sight – at Harcourt's third windmill in the 1950s, and which is believed to have been built around 1700, and ceased production in 1925.

Then into Carlton Rd., and beyond "Kibworth Cottage" out of sight in the distance, stands Kibworth Hall, and beyond that – to the east of the road – Carlton Clump, the eventual site for Kibworth's water reservoir, while due west of the clump and on the opposite side of Carlton Rd., on the land where its highest point is in "Old Mill Furlong", Harcourt's second windmill, is believed to have once stood, this also no longer around by 1780.

Water? Cloudy and Polluted Or Crystal Clear

Since the opening of the Leicester to Hitchen Railway – Kibworth became a much more important place than it was in the coaching days, when many accidents occurred, especially before the opening of the new section of turnpike, even though the traffic was light.

Here, like other places, there was a class of the old school who needed, nor desired change, what did for their fathers would do so for them, and there were people who wished to progress with the times. The attempt to repair and improve the church, was met with great opposition, mainly due to the cost, the railway company when forming the line, met with opposition in almost every field, the anti-gas school took many years before they saw the light, as was also the case with a good clean – clear – healthy – drinkable water supply.

One can only imagine what the water supply was like for the average working man before the Government introduced the Water Act in 1875, to enable everyone to have a clean piped water supply, instead of the supply they had, which can best be described when first attempting to pump water from the wells in colour and density as the same as a river in flood.

This usually cleared slightly after a bucket or so had been removed, providing it wasn't a dry period when the well would be dry in any case, or – after a period of heavy rain, when the incoming contaminated water seeping into it disturbed the whole well, with the result that the entire contents would end up cloudy and polluted, and probably the inhabitants were prepared to put up with their lot.

But by 1884 some realised they could do something about the water situation – if only they could convince the old school and those more fortunate than themselves that they wished for a better water supply, little realising at the time the many decades it would take to achieve their aim, and those that started out on the quest for pure clean water would not survive to see it achieved. In that year alone many residents in the village were in poor health, when many houses had no water for 14 weeks – caused by the dry season.

In 1900 the water supply at Kibworth was bad, when 3 out of 6 samples taken were poor, and at the 1901 census – when Kibworth and Smeeton's population was 2009, and expected to grow, the supply – even if it was pure – which it wasn't – was critical. By 1910 the council decide that no new houses will be allowed to be built unless they had a well and pump of their own.

In 1912 with the exceptional rainfall, there was an adequate supply of water, but in 1913, when the rainfall was normal there were numerous complaints. In Beauchamp that year there were 83 public pumps, and 47 houses occupied by 149 persons were without a proper supply on their premises. In addition 18 houses occupied by 70 persons were without a supply owing to the drought, some for 9 weeks, which today doesn't bear thinking about when we are advised to drink pints of water a day. While at Harcourt, the supply from the public pump at the "City" was only fit for use in the wet season, at other times 14 houses occupied by 67 people had to use the "Cross" pump, 300 to 340 yards away. This pump which at the time was supplying over 110 persons was out of order for 6 days during the drought.

Owners and tenants of 9 houses in Hog Lane were proposing to apply to pipe the water from the Cross pump, so avoiding the many treks each day, but the owner of the pump disallowed this, for if these were allowed to – then it was open to other tenants in Kibworth to be allowed to do the same, although there was water running away from the well continuously. No one wished to force a water rate on Kibworth, and if they had the water supply from Leicester, their rates would go up about 7s in the pound, and rents were high enough, a six-roomed house was 6s. 6d a week and working men protested at any increase.

The water situation had still not improved in 1914, and patience of the powers from above was running out with the villages, and notice was served on owners to provide a clean water supply for their tenants. One, where his wells were contaminated from cow sheds on adjoining property, which needed to be demolished and the manure heaps removed. The owner claimed the property on which notice had been served belonged to his mother and she had gone to great expense trying to find water, but had been unable to do so. They claimed there was plenty of water, but it was near the weir, and unfit for drinking purposes. In the end he claimed he had permission for his tenants to use the pump 55 yards away, but although he did not have it in writing to guarantee it, the situation was allowed to stay as it was and his tenants continued to suffer.

The Three Horse Shoes had a well on its own property, which had been cleaned out and rebuilt to the bottom; it now had a well – where 300 gallons an hour were coming in. They proposed to connect the overflow from that with the cross pump, which would increase the supply for the other properties, but it was not carried out.

The same year, at a heated – to say the least (and that's a major understatement at this and all meetings on the water supply) – of a joint Kibworth and Fleckney meeting to discuss the water, they were told that for 4,000 people, 60,000 gallons a day would be required. The initial cost to bring the Leicester water to the villages was estimated at £10,000, or a cost of £2 10s per head. This was considered prohibitive and Kibworth wished to withdraw from the scheme. In the end Fleckney decide to proceed and find out the probable cost and after more sarcastic heated remarks between the two parishes a committee was appointed to look into the scheme, although the following year Kibworth decided to wait until after the War.

Even after the war in 1920, the saga continued – when our three villages were told that due to the enormous cost they could not go on with the water supply at present, and the position remained the same the following year even when they were assured that the pipes would be laid free of any charge to all consumers within the limit of the supply from Leicester.

So on the saga went until September 1929, when the question of Kibworth's water, was brought to fore because there had been a epidemic of throats in the village and the water supply was pounced on, but the Medical Officer was quite positive the water was not in the least responsible for the throats. He had sampled the water, and of the 25 wells analysed, 21 were condemned. (The following year, nine samples were taken, and all were condemned as unfit for drinking proposes.) He took 15 samples, between Fleckney Rd. and the bottom of Main St., and all the samples were bad. There was evidence of sewage pollution in them all, and the simple reason why no disease had broken out, was that if people lived there long enough and drank the water long enough, the inhabitants would develop a certain amount of immunity, but all the water he had mentioned was absolutely unfit for drinking purposes. The pollution had been there for sometime, and in future they must see to the rainwater storage arrangements. There would soon not be enough water to go around, and yet there fell on every house in the year, enough to supply its want in a year, The parish council had discussed the water supply and said that when the wells were very low was not an opportune time to analyse the water and suggested the matter be postponed until a more normal time, which they considered was after rain had flushed the wells, but they did not say what the residents should do until that time arose.

Another five years went by – and in April 1934 in parts of Kibworth, some of the wells had failed after a dry period because they were not deep enough, but the residents were told there was no need to panic, there was a wonderful spring in Weir Road (even thought it was unfit for drinking purposes in 1914 and the conditions there remained the same), that could be used in case of emergency, when in fact only those fortunate enough to have wells sixty feet deep were assured of a reasonable supply of water. Mere mortals – who only had wells around 20 odd feet deep, were those suffering the most. Even these had to be shared between a number of households, and for many years past – almost from the start – the residents had divided into two groups, the "we have..." and "we want clean water".

By now though – patience had finally run out with Kibworth, as according to the Public Health Act of 1875 there should be a sufficient supply of water in the area, and the continued drought throughout the Country brought the water question to the front. It had been discussed in Parliament and the sum of £1,000,000 had been set aside for the relief of rural areas. In the north-west and northeast of Kibworth the wells had failed and residents were depending on their neighbours for water. They and the surrounding villages came within the area the Leicester Corporation were bound to supply water with – if they demanded it.

At a joint meeting of the five villages they hear that Smeeton had already held a parish meeting and their decision had been "We do not want water from Leicester, we have enough now as we have whisky for." Fleckney had asked for another joint conference. Kibworth Harcourt and Great Glen were sitting on the fence. The scheme would cost £23,000. The building of the Reservoir would cost £4,500., and the villages would have to pay the following amounts: – Great Glen £4,300, Fleckney £7,300, Kibworth Harcourt £3,800, Kibworth Beauchamp £5,800, Smeeton Westerby £1,800. In an ordinary sized house it would cost one shilling a week.

After more long – heated arguments between the "we have..." and the "we want clean water" camps, a motion with a huge majority against was carried, and the village continued to rely on its water supply from local sources. Later in November a survey on water supplies and showed:

	Beauchamp	Harcourt	Smeeton	Total
Number of houses inspected	445	142	83	670
Number of people in houses	1502	471	315	2288
Number of wells	194	61	39	294
Number of houses without water	46	13	19	78
Number of homes short	69	5	2	76
Number in favour of main supply	168	58	33	259
Number against mains supply	180	58	24	262
Neutral	89	25	23	137

One of the main interests to the ratepayers during the survey was not the effect the water had on their health but the cost of the proposed mains supply, even though many houses had been without a proper supply for eighteen months or more, others from a few weeks to six or seven months, whilst a great number have intermittent shortages varying from one day to three weeks or so. Also the distance some households had to carry water was considerable, and the results of all the water samples taken for bacteriological analysis, when only two were good in both Beauchamp and Harcourt. The reason people were short of water in Harcourt and Smeeton was that the wells and pumps were out of order, because the landlords would not go to the expense of putting them in order.

Today the results of the survey seem quite frightening, and you would have thought that more households would have been in favour of a proper supply after all the years of suffering, rather than being concerned about the cost, especially when we are advised to drink pints of water a day.

The arguments still went on with "we h..." group still pushing the view that if the parishes did not want it, it would be sheer mockery if they were told they must have it. Later the "we h..." still refusing to give up, say they would not be absolutely sure of water if they did go to Leicester, a drought would make everybody short, but were assured that if they found anything wrong it would be put it right.

The "We want" then propose to send the report to the Ministry, because if they did not send it there are plenty of other people who would, so we may as well get on with it. Yet the "we h..." propose that the matter be deferred. After further doubts whether Leicester were not selling something they had not got, they finally vote 12 to 5, to send the inspector's report to the Ministry.

At the next meeting they were effectively told to get on with it or the Ministry would instruct the County Council to do so, and in the latter case the total cost might fall on the parishes concerned, instead of being partly funded by the government. It was clear that the Leicester Corporation had the only right to supply Kibworth, Smeeton and Fleckney with water, and unless that right was waived there was no power to go elsewhere for a supply.

By now though, the cost was coming more and more into the arguments. A member of the "we want clean water", wanted to know – with regard to the heavy rate being put on the parish, what was going to happen if the workers there would not be able to pay it. If the cost was going to be put on the general rate it would save a lot of trouble.

But the council thought they should take seriously into consideration the paying of the charges out of the district rate. In many village schemes they were merely makeshift, and now they had come to a time when the job would have to be done properly, and were prepared to pay 25 per cent of the cost of such schemes out of the district rate.

At the end of another heated meeting, they agree to approach the Ministry, as to whether they would give a grant to the scheme, and if so, upon what conditions.

In January 1935 the villages hear that they would be having a new water supply there in 2 years, whether they liked it or not. Later the Leicester Waterworks state they were willing to carry out the work and the cost had gone down to £21,600, on the same terms previously stated, then finally in December 1935 they seal agreement with the Leicester City Corporation for the water supply. The scheme will include a service reservoir at Carlton Clump, and the village was assured that there would be sufficient pressure from there for Kibworth as the Leicester Corporation were insisting on larger pipes being put in at Kibworth than were used in the city so that it looked as if they would have a bigger pressure to Kibworth than in the city.

So after a period of 60 years of trying by the "we want clean, clear water group", Kibworth finally was to get a water supply.

Yet problems still rumbled on, when in September 1936, after many complained of what they considered sharp practice on the water supply charges, with residents on the side of the road near the mains supply were being charged 25s to connect to the mains, while those on the opposite side of the road were being charged £4 10s., causing grumbling among the villagers. In Weir Rd, the main had been laid on the side of the road with only 13 houses, while on the other side – were 35 houses. At Smeeton the main was on one side of the road and suddenly crossed the road to the other side, to run alongside a field, with no houses, so the residents were charged the full amount. After talks with the water company, they assure them there will after all only be one flat rate.

The water supply though was not eagerly taken up despite the conditions that must have prevailed, for the following year, tired of making appeals to the villagers at Kibworth and Smeeton to get their houses connected to the water supply, a more drastic attitude in the matter emerged, and notice was served on the residents where thought necessary. By May 1938, after receiving further applications to connect to the water supply there were only 616 households connected in the Kibworth's, Smeeton and Fleckney, and by 1943 there were still only 893 connected in the those villages.

The village and private pumps continued in use for many years after the second world war, and many wells in the three villages are still in use today, with some powered by electric pumps, although not fit for drinking proposes – at least by today's standards, and at least one house relied on the water from its own well, until the drought in 1976 forced the owner to accept the mains supply.

Perhaps now in our time of plenty, we should think of what our ancestors had to contend with, so when one is out walking through the fields – remember.

Carlton Road to Victoria Street

After our stroll through Kibworth, we find our carriages waiting to transport us to Smeeton, with Frederick himself in charge of the carriage drawn by "Jack" the horse on the left of "Kitty" the white horse.

On our way there, we pass the Old House into Main St. and the view facing us up and beyond the gated section of Harcourt Terrace. The second house from the corner is another of Kibworth's grocer/greengrocer shops and typical of those where there front room was used as the shop.

While next to and adjoining this "Harcourt Cottage", one of Kibworth's closed Inns where its name is not absolutely certain, *and is said to be the "Navigation Inn". Originally they are thought to have been built as three separate cottages for agricultural*

"Harcourt Cottage", another of Harcourt's Extinct Inns.

workers, and the right hand third – which has a cellar below, was probably the Inn, but if so, were there two Navigation Inns in Kibworth?

The "Harcourt Cottage", Navigation, along with the other Inns in Main St. that had closed by the 1840s, and all probably due to the opening of the new section of turnpike in 1810.

The Kibworth section of the canal opened in 1797, and Kibworth Grammar School, the owners of the Wistow Rd., farmland, through which the canal flowed, received £200 in 1837 as compensation for the land they lost from the Grand Junction Canal Co., that, plus another £50 that the Rev. Hildebrand the Headmaster at the time added from his own money, was spent on building a house and premises there, the Navigation Inn, now "Bridge Farm". By 1845, Wm. Barnes was the Publican until c 1861, when he also delivered the coal from the barges that off-loaded there cargo at the wharf there, to your house. After that, Harry Taylor was the Innkeeper and farmer until 1871, when he failed to appear at the Licensing Sessions and the licence was removed. So Bridge Farm was only the Navigation Inn for around thirty years or so, although he continued to farm there until 1889.

So in all probability there were two Navigation Inns in Kibworth – although not at the same time, but one can only guess the reason why landlocked Kibworth had three Inns! – with various nautical names.

While on the opposite side of the street, Henry Buttress is the Innkeeper at the Admiral Nelson, *certainly the left half of which dates back to the 17th Century,* and also according to Woodford "this was also famous at the club feasts at Whitsuntide", held in its bowling alley. Later around the time of our tour, up to a 100 used to attend the annual dinner in connection with Kibworth Oddfellows Lodge, in a first floor room, *where a large eye was painted in the centre of the ceiling, spooking the then young Anthony R. Cartright every time he went into the room, when his father Frederick kept the Inn around 1931.*

In February 1935 the licensee and owners of the Admiral Nelson (as also were the licensees of the Three Horse Shoes and the Foxhound but they improved there premises) – were told that unless they improved the premises they would be referred to the Compensation Authority, with a view to close the Inn, they didn't and the Northampton Brewery Company extinguished its licence on 20 April 1936, *and placed a Covenant on the building to stop an Inn being re-opened there in the future.*

As we glance up the hill, on the right standing on the corner, the "Old Bakehouse", then attached to that – another of Kibworth Inns, the "Fox", *built around 1740*, where William Gilbert was the publican at the time of our tour. From around 1905 the Fox and other public houses, had, at the Annual License Session been told to improve their premises. The Authority had been told to reduce the number of public houses and at that time – the Fox, was the least most rated house in Kibworth. The Inn finally closed shortly after again being referred to the Compensating Authority in February 1913 (the tenant innkeeper's received compensation when they were forced to close if the owners declined to update them) when Harry Shephard was the Innkeeper there, the Inn had been leased to James & Edward Flint, Brewers, Leics., from 1896 to the time it closed. *Then Ellen Armstrong was the tenant only there until 1918, when R. B. Haymes, the owner, sold the house to William Coleman.*

Next to and up from the Fox Inn, once stood the Harcourt's village stocks, and opposite those the blacksmiths shop, thatched cottage, carpenters workshop and yard – all also owned by the Coleman family.

St. Wilfred's and rectory, taken from the Lych-gate steps, c 1900.

Our coachman, Jack Porter, in charge of "Kitty", makes a detour via the turnpike to view the Lych-gate and cemetery, opened for its first resident in 1893. Then look at another view of the church and rectory from the turnpike, there you meet Walter Bale about to record for us another of Kibworth's long gone views, from the steps of the Lych-gate.

Moving on, then pause on the corner of New Rd., and just prior to the railway bridge which spans the turnpike – we see the allotments on the corner of West Langton Rd., which, if the proposed route for the railway had gone to plan, the line would have dissected them, therefore affecting many of the 139 villagers who had allotments there.

Then imagine the view further along from the bridge of the brickyard, buildings and clay pits (now the tip), and their reflections in the pits, by now filled with water, and where many of the local children used to go fishing. The brickyard was managed by Job Bull Woodford from around 1860, and until he retired around 1880, *then rented and run by the Woodfield family until it finally closed after Dennis Woodfield died in January 1945.*

Kibworth's Brickyard, c 1924, the photographs at least
second-generation copies, the originals it seems, the same
as the yard no longer around.

Then of the Brickyard house itself that used to stand in the hollow in the far left-hand corner, with the railway embankment at its rear.

Continuing our tour we cross the bank and then into Smeeton Lane, where the original height of the wall belonging to the Manor House, is still noticeable, compared with the new top section.

Victoria St., c 1906.

As we pass into Victoria St, and at the bend in the road, glance to our left for a now long lost view the rear of "Victoria House".

Then the house from the recreation ground gateway, with its garden and adjoining field now occupied by the health centre and the senior citizens' homes.

We then pause at the field that finally became a recreation ground after the subject first came up in March 1895, and the parish council finally manage to purchase this field in Smeeton Lane. Johnson & Barnes made a gift to the village of £300 towards the £400 needed to purchase it, the remainder came from private donations, and on Tuesday 22 May 1923, the Silver Band paraded through the village, followed by the Parish Councillors and natives, and when it reached the Recreation ground. Mr. H. T. Grant. JP performed the opening ceremony. The Band played for dancing for a record crowd, until cleared by torrential rain. In June they decide to erect a shelter at the top of the recreation ground and provide swings and see-saws for the youngsters. Thirteen years later they decided that the recreation ground was to be locked up the 1st Monday in December of each year to prevent a claim being made for a right of way!

Later in the 1950s the bottom end of the recreation ground was the location for Kibworth Rockets Cycle Speedway team, for around 10 years.

Smeeton and Westerby

Leaving Kibworth, we head for Smeeton in the spring of 1775, five years before the Enclosure Act for the Lordships of the three villages was passed, and pause at the top of the valley and imagine the scene across the open-fields, the land as we know it today yet to be divided into smaller enclosures, with hardly a hedge or ditch in sight, and with a bridge at the bottom of the dell – situated just inside Smeeton's parish boundary. Later the ditches would be constructed and hedgerows planted as the fields were enclosed.

As we travel down the hill on the bridle-way into the valley, we pass field (219) on our right and what was to become Lower Delcus, with Delkers Bridge at the bottom of the dell, which, in March 1775, the Overseers of the Highways for the Parish of Smeeton Westerby had repaired with 2 slabs at a cost of 2s. (*I assume of stone, but the type of bridge is not stated, but this and the stone bridge in Debdale Lane were probably similar to the one on the* "view from the cricket field", shown later, both of these were repaired with stone slabs around that time.) On the western side of Delkers Bridge, is field (220) now known as Delcas One.

The bridle-way is frequently underwater in the rainy season (hence the need for a bridge, but for 125 years at least there has been a culvert under the road). Part of the torrent of surface water drains from its highest point of 475 feet in field (238) near the site of Smeeton's far windmill, along the dell which forms the course of the parish boundary dividing Kibworth and Smeeton, into Delcas Two, through the dell's course into Delcas One, across the dirt-track, then on its way through Cover Close to add to the problem of the "Floodies" at the bottom of Weir Rd. The land falls 175 feet along the three-quarters of a mile or so of its route.

The remainder of the floodwater flows through Mill Gutter, Middle Delcus, across the Fleckney Rd., and eventually into "Johnny's Brook", and beyond.

The bridle-way improved at around the same time that Pinfold Lane was upgraded.

Moving into Smeeton we pass "Smeeton House", *which, originally consisted of a pair of cottages built in 1734, with the addition of the three-story front – around 1800/05.* The date when it first became a school is unknown, and possible so – with a previous schoolmaster there from the time the house was extended, but certainly by the time of 1841 Census, James Buzzard, age 26, ran a successful Boarding Academy there, with 29 male scholars, age 10 to 15 years. For some unknown reason the school is not recorded in the 1851 census. At some point – between 1855 and the 1861 census, James Buzzard moved his school from Smeeton House to Highfield House, and Miss Caroline Gimson, was the Principle at Smeeton House School – with one assistant, five female and two male pupils. At the time of the 1871 census Caroline Gimson is still the Governess there, with a head teacher, and three female pupils; age 10 to 16 boarding at the school. The last record of a school there is in a directory for 1877, and it probably closed shortly afterwards, for in 1881 Miss Gimson was living on Church Rd., Kibworth.

Then into Mill Lane, where on the left hand corner stands the old cottage, belonging to the Kings Head. The Inn was re-built just prior to it being put up for auction there in 1881. The lot consisted of the Inn, the adjoining cottage that stood on the corner of Mill Lane, adjacent yard, and premises containing about 700 Sq. yds. The bidding started at £800 but was eventually knocked down to Simeon Iliffe who had been the Innkeeper there since 1872 for £975; this brought relief to the natives who feared it would be sold to one of the three breweries represented at the sale. By August 1895 though – the All Saints Brewery were the owners, but he continued as the Innkeeper there until it was transferred to Joseph Grant on 11 April 1899.

At the time of our tour Alexander Askew had been the Publican and boot maker there since December 1905. Leaving our carriages at the Inn to be re-fuelled for our return journey, we stroll up the lane and on the right stands the new Rectory where on the afternoon of Thursday 26 April 1900 a ceremony took place for the laying of the foundation stone for the new Rectory House. The cost of the building was £1,400. Dr Marriott gave the site for the house, and Mrs. Marriott laid the corner stone of the new building.

Further up the lane but back in time – two Windmills existed until the 1860s. One, in the field (208) to our left where the footpath leading to Saddington Rd., diagonally crosses it, was sold at the Rose and Crown on 11th May 1877, together with the 2 acres of land and still a thriving business at that time, probably helped by its south-westerly position. *It is believed it was destroyed by* the gale force winds in March 1895, *and by all accounts with the miller inside (Woodford).* A slight hump, the base of the mill, on the left of the footpath in the centre of the field, can still be seen.

The fresh breeze which started on Saturday the 23rd, increased in strength, and by Sunday afternoon had developed into a furious hurricane which swept across the district. Considerable damage was caused to the Independent Chapel and manse, a house on Fleckney Rd. was completely wrecked by the chimney falling through its roof, it damaged many other chimney stacks, and cleared entire roofs of the their thatch, and uprooted many trees throughout the villages, including those on the western side of Delcas, and blocking the road for several days, it also damaged around two-thirds of the main roof to Christ Church. *The damage in the villages was so severe that the Sunday evening church services in the three villages were all cancelled, with every available person helping to clear the devastation.*

As we continue our tour, in the corner of the field (236) further up the lane on the right – the old house, and beyond that in the next field (238) stood the second Windmill, demolished long before the first was destroyed, the house itself was occupied until c 1936, then fell into a state of disrepair and all traces of it had vanished by the 1950s.

Then glance down the track dividing the two allotments, and on the left – in May 1901, Mr. R. T. Goodman gave the field for allotments to the working men of Smeeton, and ploughed the field for the first years crop.

Ten years later Kibworth Grammar School offered the Smeeton Small Holding Committee some of the land they owned which was already used for allotments off of the Gumley Rd., for £1500, but the Small Holding Committee came back with an offer of £1100, which was accepted, with an annual rent until completion.

Later in 1912, a local brick layer took the matter of the shortage of village allotments up, resulting in the Agriculture Organising Council stepping in, but it was left in abeyance until after the War, then in 1922 a committee of working men was formed. They purchased part of the field on the opposite side of the track dividing the allotments in Mill Lane at a cost of £200, and cut it into plots, which the villagers could purchase outright. To help raise the funds to pay the preliminary expenses they held a Whist Drive and Dance at Kibworth Village Hall.

Re-tracing our steps and turn right at the Kings Head, you pass the butchers shop and farmyard at the rear of "Yew Tree Cottage". Opposite that, the road that has undergone a few name changes over the years. In 1861 there were 14 households in "Corts Lane", by 1881 it was "Cobleys Lane", both named after local families, then around 1912 it became Springfield Lane.

Two-thirds of the building that stands on the left hand corner of the lane, was a grocer shop, this also became Smeeton's second Sub-Post Office from c 1902, and run by John Peberdy until c 1922, the post office then closing for a number of years until the 1940s. The remaining third (beyond the door) of the building down the lane was a Bakehouse

While at the bottom of the lane stands "Springfield Farm". *The building first started out as at least two cottages, with the left hand side the oldest, dating from the early 1600s, with the reminder dating from around 1830, they were converted into one farm house around 1900.*

While on the right – at the rear of number 4, it is said that the above brick work-shop, and typical of those used by the framework knitters at work, once stood in the garden.

As we move along Main St, *and pass the houses that were all destroyed when a spark from one of the coal fires ignited the thatch, and engulfed them all around 1930,* and later in 1935 four council houses were built, by H. Billing, Builder, Kibworth, for £1,238.

Just past those as we head for Debdale Lane stands the National School, which, when it opened in 1862 catered for 88 children. Previously, in 1833, there were three private day schools at Smeeton, although the location of the two of these is unclear.

The ground where the National School stands (now the village hall) was orig-inally sold in September 1834 to build an Arminian Methodist Chapel there, this though, only lasted a few years for a Calvinistic Chapel was opened there in May 1857, and that had closed by 1861, for in May of that year, the Rev. Fawssett pur-chased 320 Sq. yds of land and buildings on Smeeton Town Street for the use of a school, and in a later conveyance he transferred the land and building to the Rector and Churchwardens of Smeeton. It is unclear if the building first erected in 1834 was demolished or converted into the school.

Perhaps we should pause and reflect on the discipline at the National Schools at Smeeton, Kibworth and elsewhere from when they were first built in the mid 1800s, and continued into the early 1900s, when one word out of line; if you dared to smile after being spoken to; or not entering the school quickly enough when the bell was rung and the cane or ruler would be used, either across your backside or on the open palm of your hand – for what nowadays seem such minor offences, and if you flinched when about to receive your punishment – well !

The holidays over the same period, at the village schools, consisted of only 4 weeks holiday in August, 1 week at Xmas, 1 day for Good Friday and a half-day holiday only on Shrove Tuesday, Easter Monday and Tuesday. The schools also closed at 11am on the two days of the Kibworth feast, the last Monday and Tuesday in October, and the same for the Smeeton feast two weeks later on the second Monday and Tuesday in November.

Certainly up to the early 1900s the school leaving age was at your eleventh birthday, providing you had obtained the basic skills to succeed at work, if not, you had to stay on for one more year.

In 1927 the senior pupils were transferred to Kibworth, and in 1933 all the remaining pupils – except the infants were also transferred. By January 1968 the end was near, for it was costing £186 to teach each of the 12 pupils at Smeeton, and only £66 over the rest of the county. The school finally closed in July 1968.

Not only schoolchildren, *but adults were also punished if they fell fould of one of the ancient village customs and which still continued in the early 1900s, when, if they didn't conform to a well brought-up way of life, they were "panned out of the village".* An it was certainly carried out in the latter part of the nineteenth century, to a woman who hadn't treated her husband well, and the cause of him being sent to the Union Workhouse the previous day, when – on leaving the village for her former home some miles away, her neighbours engaged the service of a blind fiddler, and he – together with the local boys – who were glad of the opportunity to make all the noise they could – with their parents' pans and tea trays, and under the sight of their elders – escorted! – her from the village.

Then on the corner of Debdale Lane, another thatched cottage that stood back from the road that was demolished in 1900/01.

That made way for the four "Coronation Cottages" built in 1902. As we stroll down the lane to the Baptist Chapel, which seems to have had a chequered history. It was built around 1743, but certainly by the 1870s, only a few services were held each year, and at one – only six members met for a prayer on Sunday

Morning, the total ages of the six was over 420 years. It closed shortly afterwards for a number of years, then re-opened on the 5th May 1895, and finally closed in 1956. Next to which – the Baptist burial ground, where some of the earliest remains were laid to rest in 1767, *and adjacent to that was Smeeton's Pinfold.*

While further down the lane to the "Old Stonebridge", where the stream, a tributary to the River Welland goes under the lane, and on the land to our right and beyond, *there was until the late 1890s, a sluice-gate just up-stream from the bridge, and possibly the remains of, or at least the site of one of Smeeton's watermills, demolished many years earlier.* If you had been standing on the "Old Stonebrig" as it was also known as – many centuries earlier, from around 1315 to the 1560s at least, and glanced to your left, in a direct line from the bridge to St Wilfred's in the distance, you would have seen a watermill working away there, on the land belonging to the Manor House at Kibworth.

Retracing our steps and glance across the Main St. to Blacksmiths Lane, where on the left hand corner of the Lane, was, until it closed around 1902 – the Blacksmith's shop, the building dating from 1731 and owned by Robert Smalley. Next door – Smeeton's first Sub-Post Office, which from around 1895, was run by his daughter, Elizabeth, and her husband John Peberdy until 1902, the building, now all 33 Main St. At the top of the lane on the right until it closed between 1863 and 1871, was the Crown & Sceptre when John Stenson was the Innkeeper there.

A view looking back to Blacksmiths Lane and on the right
the grocer's shop run by Mary Woolman.

On Main St. as our stroll continues on its way towards Westerby, on the left hand corner of Debdale Lane, stands the farmhouse, the lowest half of which is of Ironstone and probably dates from the 17th Century. Then a group of what used to be four cottages – the first (62) – which although no records of it exist since the 1820s *is said to be one of Smeeton's Extinct Inns – the Queen Charlotte*, the remaining three have all been converted into one (66), the front one of these was at one time a General Store.

While opposite, a building at the rear of the farmhouse (35) *is believed to have been in use up to the 1850s* for a private fee paying day school for girls, for up to 24 pupils.

To the left of the farmyard – the green known locally as "The Bank", *where in more recent times until the late 1890s, a fair was held there and along the roads, at the time of the Smeeton Feast,* and later on a Sunday evening in August 1916 it was occupied by a large crowd of visitors, the occasion being the first outing for the Kibworth Male Voice Choir. *The house in the far left hand corner of the Bank was until around this time a factory for framework knitters on both floors.*

Just beyond the grocery shop, a farmyard wall built of ironstone containing the blocked up (in 1910) Mullioned windows of a former house.

Opposite that – four terraced houses and a high brick wall. Having reached the green, where in bygone ages when Smeeton was one of the larger villages in the district, it was the scene for the gatherings of villagers for their Stattis fair and may-pole dancing.

In the first of the two cottages lived Robert Holt, carpenter – his woodworking shop on the Pit Hill allotments. The sign on the corner of the "Old Bakehouse" (57) is for Mr Mattock's carpenters shop and saw pit, located at the rear of the Bakehouse. He lived at 63, the house on the left of the block, *the right hand side of which is believed to be the oldest part – dating from the late 1600s,* and competes with Springfield Farm as one of Smeeton's oldest houses.

At least two of adjoining cottages between the Bakehouse and number 63 are said to have been the servants quarters for the then owner of the cottage, with first floor door-ways connecting them to the main house, the only doubt is the Bakehouse, where its large ovens used to stand in the centre of the building. The baker and grocer there at the time of our tour was Alfred Higgs.

In front of these, Kibworth's Band on their way to the Whitsuntide service at Christ Church in 1891.

Before moving on – in front of you stands Westerby House, built in the 18th century, where the first Rector of Smeeton, the Rev R. Fawssett lived from the time the church was built, after he retired and until he died in September 1900.

Then after leaving The Green and number 63, it being the last house in Smeeton, we then step over the boundary that once divided the two separate villages, into Westerby, the two villages referred to as one – since 1773 at least.

Christ Church, c 1900.

Around the corner where the sand was extracted from the pits adjacent to the church *around 1893*, then the church itself, where the foundations were dug, and the corner stone laid for the Church on Thursday the 13th July 1848. It is built of Grey stone and consists of a chancel, an aisled nave of four bays, a south porch, and a north vestry. At the west end is a circular bell turret, surmounted by a spire. A large arch in the west wall of the nave suggests that the addition of a tower was contemplated at some future period. The two small bells were cast in 1848.

The Service of Consecration for Christ Church was held on the morning of the 31 August 1849, by the Bishop of Peterborough. In June 1858, at a vestry meeting they set a rate at 2d in the pound towards a new wall on the South side of the Churchyard, and a pair of Iron Gates, and they raised the remainder by public subscription. The Chancel though was not finished until late 1860, when the Rev. R Fawssett had erected a reredos of alabaster with marble sides. New oak stalls were also installed in the church at the same time.

In July 1895, a field (101) contiguous to the Rectory, was loaned by Robert Cort, where a fete was held to raise the remaining £100 required to repair the damaged caused four months previously to the main roof of the church by the gale that swept the district, and repair the ravages of time and the sagging ridge-beam, adding more timbers and completely re-tiling it, the Rev. R. Fawssett having already donated £100.

The Rev. G. Sale was the main organiser to raise the funds to purchase a new organ, installed in 1902.

Christ Church later c 1918.

Later in August 1921, they purchased an additional piece of land at the north end of the Churchyard, to extend the burial ground.

The Pit Hill allotments around 1908, where originally, a number of mud cottages used to stand until 1861 at least, when there were seven households living at the "Pitts". The cottages were probably pulled down prior to the start of the extraction of the sand there around 1886, the seam running from there back to the rear of the old Bakehouse. *The workshops were built c 1888 and demolished around 1919.*

To the left of these stands "Ivy Cottage" (built c 1890) around 1905, with Smeeton Terrace in the distance. Then as you reach the top of Pit Hill, on the left hand corner stands Brook House – previously known as Rosa Villa, and opposite that Highfield House.

An artist's "view from the cricket field" of Highfield as it was in the 1870/80s – at the time it was Smeeton's private boarding school, and it is probably taken from an advertising brochure for the school, with the artist painting the house white for the brochure. As you glance down the hill towards Gumley, the "view from the cricket field" is the second field (157) from the road on the right after you pass over the old stone "Westerby Bridge"[2] spanning the brook, itself part of the same aforementioned tributary.

The oldest part of Highfield is the rear of the house, dating from around 1840, and probably built by a wealthy grazier. It became a school after James Buzzard moved from Smeeton House between 1855 and 1861, and on the census for that year, he lived there with his wife, two daughters and a son, but with only 5 scholars. The house was extended in the late 1860s, and Mr. R. Kirby (who in 1867 owned the Commercial Boarding and Day School, 19 New Walk, Leicester.) informed the public in November 1868, "that he has reserved the House, eminently adapted for a Boarding School, which stands in a salubrious situation, and would be opened after the Christmas Holidays", and by 1871 – there were 33 scholars boarding at the school, but by 1881, the number had decreased to 28 Scholars.

It seems the decline had set in by the 1891 census, possibly due in part to the opening of the National Schools, and by then Edwin Potter was the Schoolmaster there, with his wife, one son; a scholar, and two daughters; both teachers, but they only had 9 pupils age from 10 to 17.

Around this time it changed from an all boys' school, and started to take in girl pupils, for in April 1895 the public were informed that "Miss Potter has vacancies for young ladies who would have a comfortable home. Proprietor, Mr. E. Potter". He died in 1897 and his daughter Miss Mary E. Potter then took charge. The school probably closed around 1900, for on the 1901 census, it was no longer a school. The name of the house had changed to "The Grange", and a Wool Merchant was living there.

The Smeeton village cricket team also played on the same field from 1873, when they managed to muster two teams for a friendly between the single and married men of the village, and by June 1875 there was a first and second eleven in the village, when the 2nd eleven played at home, and scored 31 and 36 in a match against Kibworth's 2nd eleven, who scored 22 and 76. In 2004 the battered remains of the cricket pavilion can still be seen in the right hand corner of the filed.

Further along the road, prior to the canal bridge, is the lay-by where they used to unload the gravel from the barges, which came from Mountsorrel for the construction of the roads. Later around 1900, the road itself was the first in the district to be treated with tar macadam, paid for by a Gumley resident, disgusted by the lack of action by the councils. Even at that time, Leicestershire's roads were reported to be amongst the worst in the Country. Glancing over the canal bridge, the second field on the right was the site for the Gumley Rd. allotments.

In the next field (185) after that – if our tour had taken place eight years previously, could be seen the Brick Yard at Smeeton, owned by Kibworth Beauchamp Grammar School, until it closed in 1881. The field was then let as farmland from June 1881, until many farmers later, in June 1898, they requested Mr. Ward to remove the shedding and hut from the old brickyard, today only part of one of the large pits that were excavated for the sand/clay remains.

"Apple Tree Cottage", c 1924.

Turning to our right we stroll along Pit Hill, and view the cottages, the first "Highfield Cottage", *was built around the 1860s, and possibly as servant quarters for Highfield House.*

Then "Pit Hill House", 26 Pit Hill, its name from when it was built around 1736, but since around 1910, it has been known as "Apple Tree Cottage", and just one of many cottages in the village that had their roofs replaced with corrugated iron on top of the remains of the thatch, and all probably re-roofed shortly after the gales de-thatched them in 1895.

"Smeeton Terrace", c 1945.

Then Smeeton Terrace, the house where the workers engaged in constructing the section of the canal and tunnel to Debdale Wharf, until it was completed in 1797 lived. The construction of the canal then ceased due to the lack of funds, until the last section from the Wharf to Harborough was re-started in 1805. Previously in 1776 a workhouse for 20 persons existed on the site, used not only for the poor of Smeeton, but Beauchamp and Harcourt as well.

Around the corner into Westerby Lane, and where, until after you pass the footpath leading back to Pit Hill, and reach the bend in the road, not a house was in sight. The first on the right hand corner as the road turns to the right was a general store, now number 11.

In front of you, the house which previously was the Cricketers Arms, where Mr. Crowdell, a butcher and farmer lived, and although he closed the Inn in 1888, the licence was renewed yearly by Mr. R. Haymes – the landowner, in case another tenant came along who wished to re-open the Inn, but the Licensing Authority finally realised 20 years later that the Inn had been closed all that while and removed its licence in 1908.

Strolling along past Rose Cottage, *built in 1756*, and the home of Joseph Higgs, the carrier in the village at this time and until the 1930s, to the end of the lane, and glancing over the stile and slightly to the left, can be seen "Mill Dam" field (155) on this side of the aqueduct, and field (195) on the far side of the aqueduct where the brook runs alongside the canal – named "Watermill Hill" in 1675, and "Watermill Close" in the 1780 Enclosure Award, suggests that at one time a watermill once stood there.

Having reached the end of our tour at the far end of Westerby, we find our carriages waiting to convey us back to Newtown.

The Return Journey

So as we journey home we reflect on the locations of Kibworth and Smeeton's Inns that still remain a mystery. In Barratt's book complied in late 1910, he mentions six "Extinct Inns".

The Crown & Sceptre is usually more often referred to, and is certainly the Old Crown. The Red Lion isn't in doubt, nor is the Navigation, at Bridge House, Wistow Rd., and unless Mrs Chris Dunkley moved house after 1908, then the Half Moon is almost certain.

Of the two remaining Inns, in 1905 Mr. H. Cox, gave his address as High St, Beauchamp, he is also on the Electoral Register there, well beyond the time Barratt compiled his book, so the Halford Arms, should be one of grocery/fruit shops mentioned, but its exact location unclear.

As for the Bird in the Hand, as stated, I may be wrong, but I just cannot see the schoolhouse being an Inn. During the research I could find no mention of them that is not mentioned previously. All these however should become clear when the 1911 census is printed in January 2012. If I'm not around at that time and I'm wrong – no doubt someone will inform me.

One of the other Inns that I found in my research is the "Dog & Partridge", in Kibworth Beauchamp. On the 1841 census, Harriet Tolton, age 30, unmarried with one daughter, Emma age 11, kept a Public House on the High St. The entry is twenty-four households down from the Newtown end of High St., and the tenth household up from the "Cross Bank", around where the Royal Oak was – its name is not on the census. The licence was later transferred at the Mkt. Harborough Petty Sessions to her (new) husband John Marvill on the 29 November 1842. The Royal Oak is not mentioned until 1853, so did that undergo a name change from the Dog & Partridge at some point between the two dates?

Two more Inns that I found, the "Crown & Anchor", in Beauchamp, and the "Baker's Arms", Smeeton, are recorded in the Leicestershire Quarter Sessions Licensing of Ale Houses Reorganisation. LRO Ref: QS 36/2/1-10. The recognisance of good behaviour required Innkeepers to have better maintenance of good order and rule within Alehouses, Inns and Victualling-houses, on a bond of £30 by themselves and a surety of a further £20 from another person, at that time. The register starts from 1753, but with only the name of the licensee and the sureties they had to guarantee. At that time as it was not compulsory, and only eight Innkeepers had agreed to be bound by the recognisance of good behaviour, or there were only eight Inns in our three villages, which is unlikely.

The actual names of their Inns are only included after 1825, and the "Crown & Anchor" cannot be mistaken for the other two "Crowns", as both the "Old" and "Rose" are also entered in the register, as are the Coach & Horses, Old Swan, Admiral Nelson, Fox, and the Kings Head.

The Innkeeper of the Crown & Anchor, Kibworth Beauchamp, was George Watts. Later on the 1841 census, a Geo. Watts age 43 is entered as a Beer Seller, at the seventh house down Victoria St. and the tenth household from the end of the street. It could either be "Victoria House", or the end of the row of the cottages opposite, and probably the latter.

The Innkeeper of the Baker's Arms, Smeeton, was George Beasley. Later on the 1841 census for Smeeton, there is one George Beasley, but his occupation is an Agricultural labourer. The entry is around where the "Green" is.

Our reflections over, as we travel up High St. nearing the end of our tour, the local children – on hearing the clatter of the carriages, ran to – and opened the first field gate for us, holding their hands out, waiting hopefully and receiving a reward for their efforts.

After a journey through many decades, from Newtown, to Beauchamp, Harcourt, Smeeton and Westerby, a distance of seven and three-quarter miles by Shank's pony and carriage, we arrive back on Fleckney Rd. and end our tour at the top of Buller St., to join the cricket team, who, with the match having just finished, and although the off licence was closed, members of the team were knocking on its side window, knowing full well the sympathetic licensee would provide them with a refreshing pint of his ale, served in jugs at $2^1/_2$d a pint to quench their thirst after their toils, and they tell you the result, Kibworth, who batted first, scored 118, while Billesdon could only reach 84 for 7 wickets, before time ran out.

Also thankful that Buller Street was still a private road, and the local Police Constable, could not, even if he wanted to charge them again, after having already done so, and was given a lecture from the Judge for wasting his time, because the street at the time was still private property and would not be adopted by the council until 1908.

For the Record

Francis Woodford was baptised at St. Wilfred's on the 17 January 1861. By 1881 he had moved to Leicester and lodging at 58 Upper Charnwood St., when he was following his maternal grandfather's occupation as a baker.

Francis Pateman Woodford married Sarah Ann Cheshire on 3 August 1888 at College Street Baptist Chapel, Northampton, at the time he was living at Duston, Northamptonshire, and his profession was a confectioner. By 1901, he had changed his occupation and working as a shoe room foreman (his farther-in law was a shoe riveter), and living at Kingsthorpe, Northampton. Around 1909 he moved back to Leicester at 115 Devana Rd., and again working as a baker.

From September of 1910, he was, through the correspondence column of the Market Harborough Advertiser, engaged in a debate with Alonzo Freeland and others on Kibworth and St Wilfred's past history. After the conclusion of those at the end of October, he continued to submit articles to the paper in greater detail than appeared later in his book, to enlighten the Kibworthians of his memories. These continued until he saw the advert for "A History of Ancient Kibworth. In preparation and will be published shortly by G. W. Barratt".

On seeing this he wrote: "Sir, – Since writing the few last remarks on the above subject, I see from an advertisement in your columns, that an history of Ancient Kibworth is to be published shortly by some "unannounced author" who, is no doubt, by quoting in extenso the authorities, mentioned in these notes, and also probably from being in a position to consult the parish records, will be able to elucidate some of its doubtful points, and obscure periods of its history. Seeing this and knowing how much more instructive and interesting a work of that kind will be in a compact form, I will not trespass any further on your space..." He continues: "I intended to have extended my remarks somewhat, and afterwards embodied then in a pamphlet form, with my own personal reminiscences, as a boy, but being in a certain extent anticipated by the forthcoming publication, I will conclude with sincere thanks to yourself for the great privilege you have accorded me in publishing them, and thereby rousing an interest in such a beautiful and interesting village as Kibworth, whose sons and daughters, I hope, will emulate the best of those who owned it as their birthplace. – I remain sir, gratefully yours, F. P. WOODFORD. Leicester, January 11th, 1911.

The publication of his "pamphlet" probably remained in abeyance for around three years, and possible it was published before the 1914 War, but certainly so by 14 March 1916, for under the heading of "Kibworth 50 Years Ago. Reminiscence by F. P. Woodford", it starts to be serialised in the paper.

From 1926 he was once again working in the shoe trade as a shoe hand. He and his wife had moved to 8 Cranmer St., Leicester, where he lived until he died in the City General Hospital on 2 December 1940, age 81. After a short service at Gilroes Crematorium on 6 December 1940, when only four people attended his cremation, his ashes were then scattered in the garden of remembrance which is surrounded by a yellow private hedge.

Francis Pateman Woodford 1860-1941

And finally I express my grateful thanks to Roger Holt and David Smith for taking the time to mull over the un-documented facts mentioned in this tour.

Roger is the great grandson of Robert Holt.

David is the son of Helen Smith (née Cooke.)

Cecil John (Jack) Porter (1879-1910), is the grandfather of your tour guide.

Frederick A. Boniface (1858-1907), is Jack's father-in-law.

Harry Billing (1879-1963), is my maternal grandfather.

Philip J Porter 1937-